You've Got to Be Kidding, I Thought This **Was** the Great Tribulation!

You've Got to Be Kidding, I Thought This **Was** the Great Tribulation!

Cathy Lechner

CREATION HOUSE

You've Got to Be Kidding, I Thought This Was
the Great Tribulation! by Cathy Lechner
Published by Creation House
A division of Strang Communications Company
600 Rinehart Road
Lake Mary, Florida 32746
www.creationhouse.com

Unless otherwise noted, all Scripture quotations are from the
Amplified Bible. Old Testament copyright © 1965, 1987 by
the Zondervan Corporation. The Amplified New Testament
copyright © 1954, 1958, 1987 by the Lockman Foundation.
Used by permission.

Scripture quotations marked KJV are from the
King James Version of the Bible.

Scripture quotations marked NAS are from the New American
Standard Bible. Copyright © 1960, 1962, 1963, 1968, 1971, 1972,
1973, 1975, 1977 by the Lockman Foundation.
Used by permission.

Scripture quotations marked NKJV are from the New King James
Version of the Bible. Copyright © 1979, 1980, 1982 by Thomas
Nelson, Inc., publishers. Used by permission.

Library of Congress Catalog Card Number: 99-76013
International Standard Book Number: 0-88419-667-4

0 1 2 3 4 5 6 VERSA 8 7 6 5 4 3 2
Printed in the United States of America

To my beloved father, Clive Ralph Rothert
1930–1999

You gave me life, you taught me to live and you showed me how to die.

SOLDIER

I just want to be a soldier in the army
of the King,
Just a good and faithful soldier who's
given Christ his everything.

I'm content to be a worker in the
vineyard of the Lord,
To hear Him say, "Well done, My
servant,"
That's all I want as my reward.

I don't want to be a superstar seeking
fortune and fame;
I am richer than this world by far just
praying one prayer in Jesus' name.

I would rather be a doorman in the
household of the Lord
Than to be that wealthy poor man who
sold his soul and bought the world.

To live a simple life for Jesus is all I
ask and all I need,
To reap a harvest if He pleases, or be
the one who plants the seed.

I don't want to be a superstar seeking
fortune and fame;
I am richer than this world by far just
singing a song in Jesus' name.

And if I die for Him tomorrow, don't
cry for me when I am gone;
Don't lay me down with tears
of sorrow;
I'm just a soldier going home.

—JIM GILBERT
USED BY PERMISSION

and

My friend, Venita Goodman
1952–1997

*You left your heart in Africa, but your love will
always be with us.*

I decided this time I would personally thank the makers of one $100 bills ...

IN MY PREVIOUS BOOK, I thanked the makers of chocolate-covered raisins for the candy's comforting ability during the long, boring hours of writer's block.

Many, many readers responded by graciously sending enough chocolate-covered raisins to cause me to hire a contractor to remove a portion of a wall from my house and lift me out with a crane.

I decided this time I would personally thank the makers of $100 bills and see if I get the same out-pouring of love!

Many people have learned to put up with me and pray for me, while others just stay out of the way when I am writing a new book. God bless you... because I am usually behind schedule!

Randi Lechner, my beloved husband of twenty-three years, you are just so smart, compassionate and understanding. I have given you plenty of reasons not to be so, but you have determined to love me as Christ loves His church. Darling, I love you!

My gorgeous mother, Rose Rothert. It has not been an easy year for you. Instead of me encouraging you, you selflessly push me upward. May God, who really understands, repay you now and in the life to come.

I cannot believe that the Lord would bless me with such incredible children: Jerusha Rose, Hannah Ruth, Gabriel Levi, Samuel Josiah, Abagael Elisha, Lydia Danielle and Hadassah Rose. Thank you for giving up your mommy again and again.

I simply could not do what the Lord has asked of me if it were not for Erin Yancey, Daniel Robinson and Sylvia Henry.

Special thanks and appreciation to our Covenant Ministries staff: Eric and Lynn Jones, Norman Spencer and Christine Christina.

To the faithful partners of Covenant Ministries whose faithful giving and sacrifice allow us to continue to cross lines, thank you.

My faithful prayer team: Ann Taylor, Jeanne Glanton, Martha Reeve, Ruth Rothert, Dorothy Parker, Thelma Ducharme and all the others whom

God wakes up in the middle of the night to pray for me. Please don't change your phone number! Norma, it took a great deal of courage to come back into my life. I missed you—thanks for obeying the Lord. This time you're back forever!

This may be rather odd, but I would like to acknowledge and give a big "God bless you" to my critics. The Lord allows critics to accomplish several things in my life. The first one is to reveal how so ungracious and unkind I can be at times. Just when I thought I was *so* incredibly spiritual. HA!

Above all else, to the One who gives me the reason to do anything! My Friend, my Brother, my King, my Burden bearer, my Comforter, my Provision, my Salvation, Healer and Deliverer...my precious Lord Jesus Christ. To Him be all the glory forever!

CONTENTS

Dear Reader:

Everywhere I turn it seems that I am confronted with people who are facing desperate situations. Incredibly, these are wonderful, stable, God-loving, faith-believing Christians who wonder, What went wrong, and where?

This book has been prayerfully, and many times tearfully, written for you, precious believer. You, beloved and precious child of God, know that going back is not an option, but also that staying where you are is intolerable. You're thinking, If I could just go back, I could fix it somehow. You need some answers. You need a word from heaven.

When we first discussed the vision of this book, it was suggested that it be totally serious, no funny stuff, no humor. Unfortunately, that has turned out to be impossible. This has been a very difficult year for me personally, and there were times when only God's grace and a good laugh got me through.

So, are tribulations funny? Not hardly! However, you are not alone in yours. Take my hand, and let's tribulate together. Prayerfully, you will identify with some of the treasures in this book and allow God's grace to help you

YOU'VE GOT TO BE KIDDING,
I THOUGHT THIS WAS THE GREAT TRIBULATION!

xvi

grow up, dust you off and enable you to press on again and again!

It's all for you, His bride.

With my love,
Cathy

Chapter
One

The Day Nothing Was
Funny Anymore

> *I had just had my fifth surgical procedure in as many months, but nothing helped alleviate the pain.*

MY EYES FLUTTERED open, and I was jolted awake. My heart seemed as if it were pounding out of my chest. Where was I? Nothing looked familiar. Was I in a motel room? Then it suddenly dawned on me that I had bought new bedroom furniture, the first in over eighteen years of marriage. It was my room.

Glancing at the clock, I could see that it was 6:03 A.M. Somehow I knew it was Saturday, March 21. Funny, I didn't really care what day it was, or even what year for that matter.

4

Slowly I made my way to the kitchen. The constant gnawing pain in my side was growing with each step I took. I had just had my fifth surgical procedure in as many months, but nothing helped alleviate the pain. It returned after each operation.

As I flipped on the kitchen light, I immediately noticed a device sitting on the counter that I knew just had to be the answer to this and every pain I had ever experienced. It was the Juice Boy 2000!

As I see it, the problem with infomercials is that these people assume you actually have the energy to put on a green nylon sweat suit...you know, the real swishy kind...and then peel, pare and pulverize two bushels of fruit and vegetables for breakfast.

I promised myself that I would juice for lunch, or maybe dinner or perhaps the marriage feast of the Lamb. (Incidentally, I hate lamb.)

Instead, I opened the refrigerator and made my selection. What could be better for me than a banana Popsicle? I paused at the scale nearby, then stepped on it, only to find that I had dropped another five pounds. Not good. You're probably saying, "Cathy, you're crazy. Losing weight is great!" Not for me. You see, I had already shed one hundred forty pounds in the last two years, and now I was beneath my ideal weight and continuing to drop too low for my health. I had no appetite, and everything tasted the same. After three bites, I wasn't interested anymore.

For twenty years my goal had been to go into a store where the regular, misses and junior sizes were sold and not have the salesperson ask me if I was buying clothes for my daughter. I desperately wanted to buy a pair of Calvin Klein jeans and have them actually fit. Now I have three pairs: a size ten, a size eight and finally a size six. The strange thing was, I was so sick that I didn't feel like getting dressed. A few years and twelve sizes ago, I would have surrendered a major appendage for a size six anything.

I finally wandered into my walk-in shower. In it sat a little bench. A thoughtful friend had bought it for me so I wouldn't get dizzy while shaving my legs and fall, cracking my head open. There it was, a little shower bench meant for old people. Oh well, at least I had shaved legs!

BUT SHE WAS ALWAYS SUCH A HAPPY CHILD

My precious mother is of the generation of mothers who were eternal optimists. She has a list of things she usually says to my adult brothers and me. I am positive she means them to be encouragements to us. She says things like, "When you are so far down, remember, you can always look up." When I think about it, that is sort of...well, stupid. What if I'm under something? What if I had fallen down a drain hole or got buried under laundry or dirty diapers? What would I see if I looked up?

Another one is, "Remember, every cloud has a silver lining." Great counsel, Mom, but I am not a cloud.

Of course, nowadays when we Rothert children get discouraged, we sneak off to a room to call "Mommy."

We were incredibly blessed to have parents who

You've Got to Be Kidding,
I Thought This Was the Great Tribulation!

6

thought that we were utterly magnificent and that all other children paled in comparison to us. Their pride in us knew no bounds. Virtual strangers would be stopped so that my parents could announce our virtues.

My mother would always tell anyone within earshot, "You know, Cathy was always such a happy baby." These folks did not really care. They were just waiting to check out at the grocery store. Slowly, they would grab their little ones and smile as they backed out the door ... and away from us!

Every time my mother would announce what a happy baby I had been, my father, bursting with pride, would follow her statement by saying, "Yeah, and she had such fat little cheeks, so red and round," with his voice trailing off wistfully.

In unison they would chime, "Now, our Stevie, *he* was a beautiful baby. Such a gorgeous head of dark curly hair! And he never cried; no, never, never, never ... but did we mention that Cathy was totally bald with fat red cheeks? We taped ribbons on her head so that people would know that she was a girl. Then there was our precious Harold ... and he truly was precious! And Steve is still absolutely adorable. Harold is an admiral or something like that now ... Anyway, he's something really important, and he never gave us any trouble whatsoever. Cathy, on the other hand, our fat red baby, once broke little Harold's arm and the child sang happy songs all the way to the hospital."

Have I turned out the way my parents had hoped? Each of us born into this world achieves some greatness, while others feel that they are a disappointment to family, friends, spouses, children and God.

If you fall into the second category, I have great news for you. No matter what is in your past, it is never too late to begin again.

I couldn't see that while lying on my bed, wracked with unbearable pain. Instead, I constantly tuned into TBN, hoping that someone would have a word of encouragement or hope for me.

Over and over I replayed in my mind the events that had led me to this place. I had ministered to hundreds of hurting people, seen miracles that would blow you away and traveled the world to teach and preach the gospel. Now I lay on my bed, unable to help myself, frustrated because I had done everything I "spiritually" knew to do.

One night was particularly bad. I slept with my tape player plugged into my ears playing praise music and with my Bible on my head. Frankly, I looked like an idiot. However, I was a sincere idiot!

The more ill I became, the more I turned to doctors. Even though my doctors were wonderful people who truly tried to help me, I often wondered if they were secretly sick and tired of me. I could just imagine them looking at each other, shaking their heads and saying, "I don't know; maybe she's psychotic. Maybe she thinks she sees the Virgin Mary."

The problem was, I was really hurting. It was not in my head. People who battle chronic pain or sickness can become severely depressed. Pain wears a person down spiritually, emotionally and physically.

So there I was, lying in my bed after my last surgery,

YOU'VE GOT TO BE KIDDING,
I THOUGHT THIS WAS THE GREAT TRIBULATION!

8

feeling horribly sorry for myself. I felt that I had liter-ally come to the brink of hell.

My intercessors, those loving individuals who sup-port me and my ministry in prayer, who I know love me, simply did not know how to pray for me anymore. It occurred to me that they might wonder if I was in some secret sin, but I didn't have enough energy to sin outwardly, much less the desire to sin secretly.

Although the prayer group never said so, I won-dered if they ever thought, *Cathy, will you please get healed so that we can pray for those who actually are lost and dying and going to hell?*

The worst experience I had happened about mid-night one week after the fifth surgery. By this time my doctor had told me not to expect a quick recovery because my body had been through so much.

Of course, my husband was away ministering at the time. I lay alone in that big bed with the wooden canopy over my head, unable to sleep. Suddenly, I felt an evil, ungodly presence in my room. I wish I could tell you that I did what Smith Wigglesworth did when confronted by Satan. He simply raised his lantern and said, "Oh, it's just you," then blew out the flame and went back to sleep.

To put it quite simply, I wasn't that spiritual.

THE ENEMY GIVES US A TRUTH TO THEN TELL US A LIE

As I lay there in the dark, painful quiet of my bed-room with that ungodly presence, a thought came to me. It sounded logical and even expressed how I was feeling: *Aren't you tired of being sick?*

Yes, I was tired of being sick, tired of being tired and tired of not being the wife and mother I wanted to be. Throughout this season of suffering, I endured seven major surgeries. With each one, the pain would relent, only to return with greater vengeance than before.

There...that was the fact Satan fed me. Next came a lie: *Don't you think your family deserves better? You aren't fun anymore. Your bathrobe has taken on a life of its own.*

Meekly and with increasing guilt I answered, "Yes, they do deserve better. At least they should have a mother who bothers to wear underwear under her robe."

With intensity, the thoughts continued to flood my mind, and the enemy moved in for the destruction—first of my self-worth and then of my value—using guilt as his weapon. *Your husband would probably be better off with another wife, and your children deserve a better mother.*

Then it came...the lie...the final thrust of the enemy: *God would understand if you just gave up. You have fought a good fight. Go ahead; kill yourself.*

Now some of you may be appalled at this revelation. "You're supposed to be a mighty woman of God!" Perhaps the greater danger you are to the kingdom of darkness, the more vicious the attacks you will encounter as God's servant. But you might not realize it at the time because you don't "feel" like much of a threat to the kingdom of darkness.

That is precisely the enemy's plan. I know that

what happened to me that night was not drug induced, because I had already finished off the bottle of pain pills.

From somewhere within me, strength and determination arose from a storehouse of God's Word deep in my spirit, and I shouted out in that darkness, *"No!"* It wasn't really that loud, but in my weakness I thought that *no* shook the house.

I literally had the thought, *Devil, if you think I'm going to die and leave my jewelry to some eighteen-year-old girl my husband will marry six weeks after I'm gone, you're crazy. And this carpet I believed God for, and my new copper pots and my garden tub . . . You can forget it. In Jesus' name, I'm not going!*

When I uttered the precious name of Jesus, immediately that evil presence, which I believe was a demon of suicide, vanished. In its place came a sweet, fragrant presence.

Although sleep did not come immediately, the intoxicating aroma of the sweet Holy One did and filled the room.

As I lay on my side in a curled-up fetal position, I felt something light brush over me. There, barely visible in the shadows, was a tall man waving his arm back and forth over my body. As his arm approached my face, I distinctly felt the brush of feathers against my cheek.

NEXT THING I KNEW, IT WAS MORNING

Up until that night I had been unable to walk from my bed to the bathroom without assistance. But by the next evening, the gnawing, relentless pain in my side had mysteriously stopped. My season of physical suffering was not yet ended, but one major battle in an ongoing war had been won. Praise God!

When my husband called me the following evening after his church service, he asked how I was feeling.

Because of my inability to share simple highlights, I began a long discourse detailing the previous night's suffering. Expecting him to immediately hop on a plane and come home to me, you can imagine my surprise when my wonderful, loving husband answered me by saying, "So, Cathy, let's think about this logically."

"Logically? Are you kidding? If I had a gun and some bullets and actually knew how to load it without being afraid of shooting my poodle or disfiguring myself and having to live the rest of my life looking hideous, I would have used it. So what do you mean, 'think about this logically'? I demand that you feel my pain."

Very patiently and with incredible kindness, my precious husband laid out, not only the plan of the enemy, but also our victorious outcome.

"Cathy, would you say that this attack last night was the worst you have ever been through?"

"Yes, honey."

"And Cathy, would you say that you were at the very lowest point you have ever been in your life?"

"Yes, honey." (I felt as if I were being cross-examined by Perry Mason.)

"So, Cathy, in other words, the devil, who was at his best, was no match for you at your worst."

At that, I swung my legs out on the other side of the bed and started shouting, "I've got it, I've got it, I've got it." Over and over I shouted it as I danced around the room.

Truth had come and set me free! The reality had sunk in that greater is He who is in me at my lowest than he who is in the world at his best!

O precious one, you may feel so alone right now. You may believe that you cannot possibly make it through your own trial. You may feel that what you are currently experiencing is more than you can bear.

Rejoice, child of God! He is greater in you at your lowest than Satan is at his greatest.

There is hope. So you think you want to die. So did I. In addition to being physically ill, I also went through a horrible time of aching and missing my father after he passed away. I knew that only death could bring us together again. But that's the big lie! If I had murdered myself, I would have been in hell and never achieved the goal of being with my daddy.

So live! I promise you the price of this book (unless, of course, it was a gift or discounted) that things will turn around. Push through the hard place, and grab Him who is your rock.

Remember what Mother says: "Behind every cloud is a silver door that probably won't open, but..." Oh well...

Just remember what Jesus said: "I have come to give you life and life more abundantly!" (See John 10:10.)

Chapter
Two

You Are Not Hopeless,
Only Helpless

> *I need Thee, O I need*
>
> *Thee; Ev'ry hour I*
>
> *need Thee!*
>
> *O bless me now,*
>
> *my Savior,*
>
> *I come to Thee.*
>> —*"I Need Thee*
>> *Every Hour"*
>> *refrain by*
>> *Robert Lowry*
>> *(public domain)*

"**G**OD, WHERE ARE YOU?" I pounded my fists foolishly against the shower wall as I cried. The water poured over my face, mixing with my tears. Yet, all the water that streamed out of that spigot onto my body could not wash away my sorrow.

It had been a season spent in a cave. I often wonder if we stay in the cave much longer than the Lord ever intends for us to stay. Due to our lack of hope, we tend to get used to cave life.

The incredible pain recurring in my body would go

away, only to return again and again, which only added to the doctor's prognosis that said, "All that can be done was done; you will have to live with the pain." That prognosis was not acceptable to me. Living in pain was not an option, but what was the alternative? I had a family, ministry, obligations and a huge budget, so stopping was out of the question. I had less than two weeks to recover and prepare for a big conference, and I could not even walk from my bed to the bathroom without experiencing pain.

Every day I meet Christian people who live with pain every moment of their lives. They deal not only with physical pain, but also with emotional hurts and wounds, grief, fear and despondency. People who live in constant pain eventually become so weary that they often open the door to depression. Pain can and will wear you down. But of this I am certain: God wants us to be free!

As I described earlier, my dear husband called me from the city where he was ministering and asked me how I was feeling. Having just had surgery one week prior, I felt terrible. Then Randi prophesied to me via the telephone and declared, "God is going to condense time for you. In the past, God sent the plowman, then the sower and then the reaper, each in his own season. Now God is going to speed things up. The plowman, the sower and the reaper will come more quickly so that what took years to accomplish will now only take months. That which used to take months will happen in weeks, and what took weeks will be replaced by days."

"But honey, the doctor told me that it would take months to recover from all the surgery, drugs and anesthesia. He said I may never fully be rid of the pain." I was hopelessly exasperated. I will admit it was partly because I was extremely pitiful. And Randi . . . well, he was full of faith!

When the truth of what Randi said that night sank in, I jumped off the bed and began to shout, "I've got it, I've got it!" It was so plain. I could not heal myself anymore than I could save myself. God just wanted a yielded and willing vessel.

That was one of those days marked by God! He will do that for you when you surrender totally and give Him the praise. I danced all around the floor of my bedroom, shouting and worshiping God.

The next thing I did was lay hands on those around me who were caring for my needs during my bouts of illness and command any spirit of infirmity to leave them; I released the healing power of God on their minds and bodies. It was not very long before we had a party in my bedroom. We turned on the CD player and the children joined me as we danced (I half danced, half limped) to the music of the song "The River Is Here."

What a sight we were. We must have resembled the four lepers who dragged themselves to the besieged city looking for a miracle.

After that, my strength increased daily. Actually, it seemed to happen hour by hour, just as Randi prophesied to me. God seemed to condense time and to repair my body rapidly.

20

Did I ever have doubts or setbacks? Of course I did. I would not be truthful if I didn't tell you that every once in a while a sudden, stabbing pain would come out of nowhere and the enemy would say, "See, you're not healed. It was all in your head. You are not a good enough Christian to get healed. You don't pray, fast or read your Bible enough."

During those times I would literally put my hands on my head and scream, "No, Satan! I refuse to argue my commitment to my Lord with you. The blood of Jesus and His Word testify against you. Besides that, you are a liar!"

My precious friend, you must decide *before* the trial, *before* your tribulation, *long before* you find yourself in a crisis, that no matter what:

- God loves you.
- He has an awesome plan that you may not see right now, but He is working out a phenomenal miracle just for you.
- The Lord did not single you out just so He can see how long you can suffer.
- Yes, you would look better with twenty pounds off your backside and thighs, but you can think about that next Monday (or the Monday after that, or the Monday after that...).

The biggest lie that Satan has ever perpetrated against mankind is that King Jesus never defeated him and led him captive. You say, "Cathy, if Satan has been taken captive by Jesus, then who is running around stealing, killing and destroying?"

It's like some Japanese soldiers from World War II. Long after the war was over, they had been isolated on an island and had not heard the news. Years later they were still fighting a war that not only was over, but that they had lost!

"It is finished!" Jesus cried. He won the battle, even though demons and principalities are still trying to fight a lost war.

In order for me to successfully impart to you a sense of victory concerning your trials, I must, with the help of the Holy Spirit, establish in your heart and mind the truth of the finished work of the cross.

Jesus was so incredibly exasperated with His disciples when they displayed a similar lack of understanding in other circumstances. Sure, there are times when God, in His infinite grace, sovereignly appoints miracles for someone who seems to do everything wrong.

But as far as I am concerned, Jesus expects me to use my faith in the Word, the prophecies given to me and even my will to break through.

If I had continued to lie on my sickbed after the "word of revelation" was spoken to me, I could have still been lying there a year later. (What a horrible thought...me in my Winnie the Pooh pajamas stained with last week's pizza and with really, really greasy hair.)

As you read this, you may feel that what I've described is exactly where you are right now. Your situation looks hopeless, and the enemy has exaggerated his power and diminished God's. If you will stand up right now, lift up your hands and begin to worship God, the chains of despair will fall at your feet!

Perhaps this question is running through your mind as you read: *How long does it take God to turn my situation around...a week, a day, an hour?* No, in just one moment He can change your life entirely. (Oh, if only He would do that with our hips and thighs!)

What enemies are hindering your victory?

ATTITUDE MAKES THE DIFFERENCE

Have you ever heard the famous saying, "Your attitude determines your altitude"?

I once read a story about a group of people who were determined to climb a particular mountain. No one had ever succeeded because the conditions were beyond human capability of withstanding.

The higher they went, the slower they climbed. As the journey progressed, one by one, men began to drop out and, with sadness, turn back.

They had spent years planning, raising money and making precious preparations as they lived, slept and talked about the climb. They were consumed by their dream. Although they knew that they were risking their lives to reach the top of the mountain, it was worth it all to them.

Now, even though they thought they had planned for every conceivable problem, the unpredictability of the journey caught them off guard. Several of them turned back, bitterly disappointed. Two died. Another lost fingers, toes and his nose due to severe frostbite, barely escaping with his life.

Finally, only two of the men gasped for oxygen and huddled in a tent on the side of the mountain. Caught in an unexpected, blinding ice and snow storm, they took videos of each other. They wanted to capture what they thought would be their last words... as a legacy to their families.

Miraculously, those two lived. They brought back hard-won knowledge and wisdom and once again began to assemble another team to climb the mountain.

I honestly don't get it. Of course, just standing on the top of a three-step stool makes me dizzy and nauseous. In order to entice me up a mountain, you would have to promise me that I would receive an angelic visitation and that a box of money and several pounds of fudge were waiting at the top.

Just like those climbers, we can plan and prepare and do everything right. However, life is filled with things that we never learned about in Sunday school, Bible school, or "Training for Reigning" class.

The majority will not make it, simply because it is not easy. Much of our success depends on fortitude, but most of our ability to survive is rooted in attitude.

Just a pebble in their boot is enough to make some turn back. Suffering does not *create* your spirit. Suffering only *reveals* your spirit.

A while ago I was invited to speak in Sydney, Australia, where I was to be the first speaker on the first night of a two-week conference.

It seemed as if ten billion delegates from almost two hundred nations were gathered together, waiting for the start of the conference.

Hiding my nervousness, I followed my dear Australian friend and National Youth Director, Christine Caine, as she led me, my mother and my daughter Jerusha through the overflow crowd to a waiting elevator that would take us up to the pastor's office and lounge.

Did you ever have a really humble, secret fear that if "it" ever happened, you would go crazy? No? Well then, I will share my experience with you so you won't feel left out.

The four of us were in a small, concrete, enclosed elevator when it suddenly stopped. We were trapped! My friend Chris began frantically pushing all the buttons, but we didn't move. Panic started to rise up in my throat, and all my phenomenal sermon notes fell to the floor. The praise and worship had started, so of course no one could hear me screaming.

I looked up at the trap door in the ceiling that says, "Do not under any circumstances, including death, try to open or climb out of this hole." Being the brave soul that I am *not*, I began removing my shoes as a first step in planning my escape attempt.

It seemed that the oxygen supply was dwindling, and I wondered how long it would be before we were missed. Oh no! What if this was one of those services in which the power of God begins to move during worship, and they forget that they have a speaker?

At this point, I thought it would be a good idea to

do a pat-down search on everyone for drugs. The best I could come up with was some nitroglycerin in my mom's purse. I wasn't exactly sure what it would accomplish in my case, but anything would do in an emergency.

After what seemed like hours (actually, it was about ten minutes), we were rescued. Would you believe that we were on the floor where we intended to get off, but the doors wouldn't budge? (How was I to know that?)

After we described the terrifying ordeal to Senior Pastor Brian Houston, who also happens to be the owner and operator of said death trap, he calmly said, "Oh, all of our speakers get stuck in that elevator." I laughed nervously, but I walked down three flights of steps to the sanctuary.

Sometimes it's hard for us to accept how little it takes to make us throw away the Word and turn to our "natural" reactions.

The elevator scenario was one of my worst nightmares that had happened, and yet I did not die. My friend Chris kept telling me that the elevator does that all the time and that she had been stuck on it before. She assured me that there were maintenance men who would be watching for the car...it was part of their job, and they would get us out shortly. Why didn't I find comfort in those statements?

Chris Caine had made the journey before and was there to reassure me. Had I listened, I would not have been found on the floor, hair smashed, clothes wrinkled, clutching a bottle of nitroglycerin. Some great speaker, don't you agree?

Have you ever found yourself on a journey that you carefully planned, prepared for and worked out all the problems ahead of time...and you still wound up in a crisis?

Remember, there is Someone with you who has already made the journey, fought the devils and secured your victory. It's only a matter of shortened and condensed time until you are through!

Chapter
Three

Wilderness?
What's That?

> *Often when I am reading a book and there is a scripture verse printed . . . sometimes I sort of, well, skip over it.*

*T*HUS SAITH THE LORD: **THIS is a season of breakthrough for your life, your family and for the church.**

Thus saith Cathy: "Break" is the first part of the word *breakthrough.* Isn't that special?

Often when I am reading a book and there is a scripture verse printed (don't tell anyone I do this), *sometimes* I sort of, well, skip over it. Because as a man (or woman) soweth, that shall he also reap, I ask for mercy and beg you to read the following scriptures so that this chapter will make sense to you.

And all the congregation of the children of Israel journeyed from the wilderness of Sin, after their journeys, according to the commandment of the Lord, and pitched in Rephidim: and there was no water for the people to drink. Wherefore the people did chide with Moses, and said, Give us water that we may drink. And Moses said unto them, Why chide ye with me? Wherefore do ye tempt the Lord?

—EXODUS 17:1–2, KJV

A few years ago, God began to do a wonderful, awesome thing in the earth. Some simply called it "revival." However, it was so much more than that. God was using simple men, women, teenagers and little ones to bring a simple message. The result changed households, nations, governments—both the great and small!

Mass salvations, signs and wonders, miracles, and unusual but holy manifestations were occurring in cities and churches of God's choosing. Thousands of people, hungry and searching for more of God, caught the first plane, train, bus or carpool and headed to the nearest place of visitation.

Upon arriving, seekers would stand in line for hours in all kinds of weather, waiting for the doors to open. Many were turned away because there was no more room inside.

Because many compared this move of God to a mighty river flowing in what had been dry ground, an underground, secret language began to emerge among seekers.

"Are you in the river?" was one catchy phrase familiar to those caught up in the waters of revival.

Let me put your mind at ease. I love this present move of God. I have absolutely no problem with manifestations—that is, unless you begin to slither. Then we really need to talk.

I saw many wonderful Christians, young and a little older than young (my mother made me say that), whose lives were completely and radically changed by the waters of revival. Unfortunately, many returned to their home churches and immediately began to criticize their particular "Moses" (pastor). Instead of the mountaintop excitement of songs like "Sweet Wind" and "The River Is Here," they were suddenly brought back to the valley of "This Is the Day" and "Love Is the Flag Flown High."

The same believers who shook with revival fire just the week before were now shaking a finger in their pastor's face, criticizing him for not "being in the river." One dear couple, who really loved their pastor, suggested taking an offering to send him and his wife to dip in the river "because the church was, frankly speaking, very dead."

The problem with the revival river dwellers is that, three days after they are home from the river conference, they are thirsty again. It is not your pastor's fault. God never intended for you and me to quench our thirst at another's well.

Jesus told the woman at the well that if she drank the water that He would give her, she would *never* thirst again.

Being in the river is swell. Just take another drink. But I do believe that God has a higher order for us.

A friend whom I had not seen in a long time greeted me with this question: "Cathy, have you been in the river?"

My response was, "I don't know if I am 'in' the river, but I do know this: The river is in me!"

It's great to float along in the glory river, but too many stand on the banks around us dying in a dry and barren wilderness for us to ignore them.

Do you remember the old Pentecostal chorus we used to sing? (Directions: Sing only on Sunday night because Sister Prayer Warrior might get too excited.)

> *I've got a river of life flowing out of me.*
> *It makes the lame to walk and the blind to see,*
> *Opens prison doors, sets the captives free.*
> *I've got a river of life flowing out of me.*
> —*Author: Last seen heading for the river*

WHOSE IDEA WAS THIS?

I love Exodus 17:1. The journey into the wilderness was God's idea. Imagine that! The Word says it was "according to the commandment of the Lord" (kjv).

When God is involved in your journey, it means you are going somewhere. You are moving. Obeying God means there is action involved!

God took the children of Israel straight into the wilderness, but He also said, "I will stand before you there on a rock" (Exod. 17:6, NKJV).

The reason I can trust and be at peace while going through a battle is because I know that my loving Father has gone on ahead of me. I know that if I lift up my eyes, I can see Him who not only *stands* on a rock, but who also *is* my rock.

Maybe when you went to bed last night everything was great. Then you woke up this morning to find out that the bottom had dropped out of your world. Let me assure you, nothing has changed. Your God knew last week, last month, even last year, what you would face today. Although He didn't keep you *from* it, He will keep you *in* it!

Someone once said that if God permits in His wisdom what He could have prevented with His power, it is for this purpose: that we would bow our knees and say, "Yes, Lord, Your will be done."

I have had to walk that out many times over the years, but never has my faith undergone a trial of fire, as it has this past year. After a valiant, eighteen-month battle, my wonderful daddy left this life and began his eternal one. My father and I always had a special bond. We were close and enjoyed a mutual love of the ministry, missions, music, the sea, bad jokes, chocolate, lobster ... and my mom.

For years I have heard different ones share wonderful stories regarding the loss of their loved ones. Many told of glorious funerals where many got saved and how life went on with no grief.

Until the day my father drew his last breath, we believed that he would be healed. Many times I knelt

You've Got to Be Kidding,
I Thought This Was the Great Tribulation!

36

by his side and held his hand, kissing him and wiping my tears from his face.

As we stood alone in that hospital room beside his lifeless body, it seemed as though my prayers had gone unanswered in my darkest hours and prophecies were left unfulfilled. Didn't God care? I resisted the doubts that flooded my heart, as my mother and I chose to lift our hands to heaven and thank God for giving us a wonderful husband, father and friend.

I have known the loss of a friend, but I have never had to face the loss of my faith. I knew that my dad was in heaven and that he was with Jesus. The Word tells us that to be absent from the body is to be present with the Lord. (See 2 Corinthians 5:8.) I knew all the religious things to say. At the viewing, I nodded my head in agreement with fellow believers that yes, Daddy was in a better place, and yes, I was glad he wasn't suffering anymore.

But in my heart I could not imagine life without him. Everything reminded me of him. Forgetting, I would tuck something in my heart to share with him later. I cried when I heard his favorite song, when I looked at his picture and when I reached for the phone to call him, only to remember...he's not here.

Trying to find answers, I cried out to God. I had to still my mind constantly with the Word as the attack on my faith continued relentlessly. There was a season in which I did not want to pray for anyone with cancer because of my struggle to overcome doubt and unbelief.

Many saw my struggle, and in their somewhat

misguided attempts to help me, they scorned me for my sorrow. They too had lost a father, and I just needed to "get over it." They had danced at a child's funeral, so what was wrong with me?

Before you judge me too harshly, let me first minister grace to those who are reading these pages right now and who are hurting.

Everyone responds differently. How close was the person to you? What else was happening in your life at the time? Yes, that person was born again and is in heaven, but what about the place he or she occupied here? How do you make the hurt go away? What about birthdays, Father's Day, Christmas or the anniversary of your loved one's passing?

After many months of agonizing, searching the Word, seeking counsel, accepting rebuke and finally pulling myself up and going on, I came to the end.

My husband gathered the children and me and took us to a quiet house on the Gulf of Mexico. There, away from the phones, fax machines, cell phones, computers...in the quietness of my surroundings, the Lord visited to me.

I had just come in from swimming, had taken a shower and had fallen exhausted on the bed. My body was tired, and my head hurt. Randi, my wonderful husband, came into the room and opened the window so I could hear the ocean. Then he pulled up the covers and tenderly tucked me in. I felt as if I were eight years old, and it was wonderful. The smell of the air and the feel of the soft pillow under my wet hair were comforting.

Somewhere between awake and asleep, my Lord spoke—not audibly, but I know I *heard:* "Cathy, you are angry with Me because I took your father."

I began to sob, turning my face into the pillow. What was so incredibly moving to me was the tenderness of His voice . . . so gentle, so loving.

Was it true? Was I angry with my Lord? But I trusted Him. I loved Him. Everything I did and every decision I made was for Him.

That is the difference between faithfulness and loyalty. I had been *faithful,* but in my heart I had not been *loyal.* I would never commit spiritual adultery against Him, but I was harboring unforgiveness and was guilty of disloyalty.

"I'm sorry, so sorry, Lord. Please forgive me. You're right. I have been angry. I accused You of not upholding Your Word. You never lie." The words tumbled out, and my tears, which had been bitter for so long, began a cleansing, washing away the grief, hurt and loneliness.

"I miss him, Holy Spirit."

"I miss you, Cathy."

"I believed for him to be healed. I told everyone. I look like an idiot."

"Daughter, your dad, My faithful son, was tired and wanted to come home. He asked me to take him. And I honored his prayer—not yours."

I don't know when, but Randi heard my sobbing. Without saying a word, he had slipped his arm under my head and held me while I wept. Emotionally exhausted, I curled up next to my friend, my lover, my husband and fell into a sound sleep.

Randi's action was a valuable lesson to me. There are times when wounded or grieving people don't need our testimonies, our opinions or even our favorite Scripture verses. Sometimes a wounded heart just needs a shoulder, a pillow or a friend to hold her through the darkest night, without checking a watch, cell phone or voice mail.

Was it just me, or was the sun brighter the next day? The air smelled fresher. Even the children's high squeals of laughter and their fourteen bare feet running through the house didn't bother me.

The chains of my self-inflicted prison were open, and I walked out free.

Trials come. Tribulation is supposed to work patience. Joy will eventually follow nights of weeping. Still, we need a road map, because there are times when we lose our way in this noisy, busy and complicated world in which we live.

Friend, I love you. I may have never met you face to face, but even as I sit here writing, my heart is moved with the compassion of the Holy Spirit.

Jesus loves you. If you have lost your way, He has provided a road map in His Word. Take His hand (and mine too if you think that will help). You are not going crazy; trust Him to bring you out. I did . . . and just see how faithful He was to me.

Keep reading, because in the next chapter, we will navigate the wilderness together and come out into His plan.

Chapter
Four

Where He Leads Me I Will Follow, As Long As I Can Get Room Service

> *Randi was*
>
> *in Belgium*
>
> *ministering, and*
>
> *I felt alone sitting*
>
> *there, holding my*
>
> *half-conscious*
>
> *son as he burned*
>
> *with a fever.*

IT CAME ON US WITHOUT **warning. That is usually the devil's way. Why are we so surprised when it happens?**

Tuesday afternoon found me at Wal-Mart picking up a few last-minute things before I had to leave for Australia. Hearing my purse playing the tune "Au Claire de la Lune," I began the frantic search for my cell phone. Women's purses are rightly named "the black hole." I found my wallet, sunglasses, eyeglasses, lipstick holder, five hundred Altoids that had spilled in the bottom and, finally, my phone. But by then it had stopped ringing.

My four-year-old, who knows more about these

phones than I do, got my voice mail. It was my son's teacher calling to inform me that Gabriel was spiking a fever and his left eye was swollen shut; would I please come and get him?

Two hours and one doctor's visit later I was rushing my little guy to the hospital. Randi was in Belgium ministering, and I felt alone sitting there, holding my half-conscious son as he burned with a fever. The doctors threw out a couple of possible diagnoses, including spinal meningitis, which could take his life in less than two weeks.

I never left my son's side. I slept fully clothed by his bed, held him down while IVs were inserted, made surgical glove balloons while they drew blood for more tests. Finally, I was told that Gabriel had a condition that could affect his brain and his sight. He needed to be on heavy-duty antibiotics, administered through a tube, for at least two weeks. And of course, he had to remain in the hospital for the whole ordeal.

Now another problem loomed large before me. My five-year-old son was very ill and needed me to stay with him, but I also was scheduled to leave for a conference in Australia. In my mother's heart there was no question about what decision I would make...my son came first.

I was just about to make the phone call to cancel my trip when it seemed as if my finger got stuck on the number keypad. Once again, that same sweet voice that I have become so familiar with said, "You did not ask Me."

Since God already knows everything and nothing is

hidden from Him, it is ridiculous to argue. So I asked Him, almost fearing the answer. He replied, "This is a distraction from the enemy. You are to go to Australia."

Immediately thoughts and questions popped into my mind. *What will people think? If I tell them that God told me to go, I can see the raised eyebrows, the looks of "I can't believe you're actually thinking of leaving your son" and the Pharisees licking their lips as they begin to gather the firewood.*

Quietly and deliberately I continued my preparations to leave. It seems that in my life 99 percent of the battle is enduring until the breakthrough comes. When my husband called from Belgium, I carefully laid out all the details, Gabriel's prognosis (slow, but improving) and my heart-wrenching decision. His counsel? You guessed it!

"Honey, you know God wants you to go, so either go and be fearful and miserable, or go in trust and faith, rejoicing." I was tempted to tell him that I believe I still had family in the Mafia, but I knew he was speaking truth. So, as much as I dreaded it, I resigned myself to going and grabbed my crocodile-wrestling outfit to throw in my suitcase.

DOOR NUMBER ONE OR DOOR NUMBER TWO?

We know, as men and women of God, that the wilderness is one of the stages through which we must go for our development. If you keep binding and rebuking your wilderness and it doesn't go away, it just might be God!

God does what He has been doing since the beginning of time. He is doing it today . . . and He gives us a choice, just as He did the children of Israel.

Exodus 17:7 says, "He called the place Massah [proof] and Meribah [contention] because of the faultfinding of the Israelites and because they tempted and tried the patience of the Lord, saying, Is the Lord among us or not?" The children of Israel were in the wilderness according to the design and plan of their Lord.

That spot was given those two particular names because the people had to make a choice there. Two spiritual principles were being laid before them: *Massah,* meaning the "proving of God to go in and possess," and *Meribah,* which means the "contention of God or contending with God."

Please allow me to take you on a little discipleship journey that leads up to this place of decision. Every battle we fight and overcome is simply preparation for the next larger battle that we will hopefully stand and overcome. Unfortunately, the children of Israel had a pretty lousy track record.

In the Old Testament, water always speaks of the dealings of God. From the descriptions of how the children of Israel passed through water, we can glean insights of how God wanted to deal with His people.

WATERS OF SALVATION

Lift up your rod and stretch out your hand over the sea and divide it, and the Israelites shall go

on dry ground through the midst of the sea.
—Exodus 14:16

Moses lifted up the wooden rod, which represented the cross, and they declared, "There is a way through that which was impossible." God crushed the power of great Egypt, and the Israelites started on their discipleship journey. Here we see that we can't go anywhere in God unless we first experience the waters of salvation. If you have never made Jesus the Lord of your life, then I encourage you to do so now.

DOES THIS WATER TASTE FUNNY, OR IS IT JUST ME?

When they came to Marah, they could not drink its waters for they were bitter; therefore it was named Marah [bitterness]. The people murmured against Moses, saying, What shall we drink? And he cried to the Lord, and the Lord showed him a tree which he cast into the waters, and the waters were made sweet. There [the Lord] made for them a statute and an ordinance, and there He proved them.
—Exodus 15:23–25

Remember, we're talking about God's dealings in our lives. These are the waters of restoration.

Every one of us who has come out of Egypt after experiencing the power of the cross comes to the realization that he or she has some bitter waters in his or her life. *Everyone.*

Many of you have had someone in your life who said

to you, "I don't want you anymore," "I don't want this marriage" or "I don't want you in my church, job ..." The list goes on.

Among these bitter experiences that God desires to make sweet are hurts, broken hearts and feelings of rejection. Some Christians are still camped out at Marah, thinking that is the normal Christian life. When you see them coming toward you at church, you try to avoid eye contact. Too late! They head straight for you, and you make the regretful mistake of asking, "How are you?"

"Well," such a Christian begins pitifully, eyes downcast, "the doctor says I have pus pockets in my throat and, excuse me (hack, hock, spit, cough), it's turned puce, which means I'll probably gag all during my solo this morning." You're thinking, *This is much more information than I need to know,* as you assure her that you will put her pus pockets on the prayer chain. She adds, "Please do that, and remember my yeast infection, too."

THE WATERS OF CONSOLIDATION

> And they came to Elim, where there were twelve springs of water and seventy palm trees; and they encamped there by the waters.
>
> —EXODUS 15:27

"Thank God, we've arrived!" After years of desert living under that blazing sun, with no water and then bad water, finally, everything came together at Elim.

At Elim were twelve springs of water. Twelve represents governmental authority. Here God begins to bring right order into your life. You discover that sub-mission isn't such a terrible thing after all. Submission is more than a cop-out when a salesman wants to sell you a freezer full of meat. "Well, I'll have to submit it to my husband." You and the salesman both know that you are not even going to ask your husband.

God brings right order into your walk and stability into your priorities. That's what happens at Elim. And oh, girlfriend, think of it—seventy palm trees! What a wonderful place to be. Seventy represents the scribes who wrote the Word of the Lord. They had great teaching, great preaching and awesome worship.

They have a great ministry team, a Bible school, a day care, a Plexiglas pulpit and ten lovely, though somewhat inexperienced, dancers. The flags of the nations hang around the church with the four mam-moth banners that Sister Ima Craft made and donated. Everyone pretends not to notice that the Lamb of God on the throne looks more like Foo Foo the toy poodle with a plastic crown from Toys R Us glued to its little cotton-ball head.

We have now begun to look like a successful twenty-first century, conference-gathering church. So what is wrong with that, you ask?

When God begins a new season in the church, He begins it simultaneously in individuals...in you.

I wish we could stay at Elim forever. We could wor-ship for hours back there. Elim was never given to the children of Israel as the end of the journey, though; it was just a stopover.

I don't know what your city is like, but mine has

YOU'VE GOT TO BE KIDDING,
I THOUGHT THIS WAS THE GREAT TRIBULATION!

50

churches everywhere—on almost every block. You can find churches downtown and uptown; there are river churches, seeker-sensitive churches, cult churches and inner-city churches.

They used to be filled with a care group of hungry believers who met in a storefront, excited, full of vision and praying continually. Then God blessed them, gave them property, miraculously provided for a building, paved the parking lot and dropped into their laps a sound system that came from the Rolling Stones. We've arrived at Elim.

After the momentum wears off, many precious saints begin to look around and say in their hearts, *Is that it?* Slowly, the church begins to lose and gain members from other area churches, and the pastor works like crazy in order to maintain Elim. Hundreds of churches throughout the world have thought that Elim was the final will of God.

God has something more for this planet!

Chapter
Five

OK, God, I'm Willing
(I Think)

> *You may be walking through a challenging season that you've never before experienced.*

WE ARE NOW BACK TO **where we started in Exodus 17:1. God, according to His commandment, takes everyone from Elim into the wilderness.**

But I don't understand. Why leave Elim? The blessings are flowing, the teaching is good, the house is nice and the palm trees sway in the breeze. And now God shocks us by telling us to move on!

Where does God take us? He leads us straight to Rephidim, where there is no water. That's not fair. Why would God take us from wells and palms to Rephidim?

YOU'VE GOT TO BE KIDDING,
I THOUGHT THIS WAS THE GREAT TRIBULATION!

56

EVERYONE HAS A REPHIDIM

Every believer who has walked with Jesus for any length of time will have a Rephidim. You may be walking through a challenging season that you've never before experienced. Perhaps you have been binding the devil while all the time it has been the commandment of the Lord.

God has commanded His church to come into this season because He wants to take us from under the palm trees where we've gotten soft, fat and flabby *and go on a journey of conquest.*

I know from experience that an overwhelming desire to stay at Elim is in all of us. You see, religion loves to settle down. Within all of us is the desire to get to a place where we say, "Oh, this is wonderful. I love my church, we are busy in the community, we are touching the people around us and we saw four individuals saved in the last quarter."

You make a decision to plant a few more palm trees, dig a few more wells, learn some new worship songs...and then God decides to move you.

Rephidim is the place where there is no water. Do you realize that if you follow God, He will take you into some challenging places? If you really want to do something for God, He will take you up to the high places.

Actually, *high places* is just a nice, soothing name for the *hard places.* It's above the tree line where nothing grows but dirt and rocks. You know that no one would come to your church if you sang, "Let's go up to the *hard* places." You also know that those are the places where you break through and see the greatest victories in God.

I am sure that out of three million plus Israelites, there were some who did not want to move when the fire and cloud did. "Oh, Jacob, I just enrolled the kids in Elim School of the Pentateuch. We can't leave now. They will wind up on drugs and have to get therapy for their dysfunction. We'll have to go on the Moshie Ruben Show.... The chickens are hatching; the baby is crawling..." Fine, throw them in the wagon, and let's go.

The cloud represented their protection, their covering and their provision. To stay behind was certain death.

God is moving us by commands, not suggestions. We have a job to do. We're on a mission. We have a world to conquer. We have the lost to bring in. We have our cities to purge and cleanse, renew and restore. These things will never happen if we just sit under swaying palm trees sipping little charismatic cocktails.

Come on, friend, let's finish this thing. Elim is great, but after a while, the challenge is gone and boredom sets in.

There is a whole land out there just waiting for you, if you will keep going. Nations are out there that will come under the anointing if you will run with God.

So that brings you to your choice. Are you going to call this place "Massah," where you prove God and go in and possess His promises? God wants to prove

You've Got to Be Kidding,
I Thought This Was the Great Tribulation!

58

Himself to you right now. In the hard places, in the trials where everything seems unfair, God is shaping you to possess greater things than you have ever known. This is not the devil's hour; this is God's hour.

What is happening right now is not the devil's plan, but God's plan, so that we can grow up and put a sharp edge to our spirit. God wants to bring forth a strong people. Beloved, some of you have been going through the fire. Rest assured, it is only a season.

You will have to make a choice. Will it be Massah, the proving of God, where you say, "O God, shape me. Prove me, please! This is a tough one, but I know You can do it in me." Or will it be Meribah? "God, what are You doing? Devil, get away from me. God, I bless You; devil, I hate you."

We often get confused. We're not sure anymore if God is for us or against us. We begin to grumble, saying, "Meribah, Meribah," until our mouth is filled with the dust of defeat.

I have heard seasoned believers and pastors say, "I don't know what is happening. We had more people in our church a year ago. Our finances are down. The holy prayer ladies told me that there is probably a curse over the place because someone spilled a full communion cup last Sunday. One intercessor said that when she squinted one eye and lifted her left knee, the flag of Hulumbooger and Kulumbooger resembled the head of a pig! Maybe that's what is wrong!"

GIVE US A BREAK!

It is written that the steps of a good man are ordered of the Lord! (See Psalm 37:23.)

God is not taken by surprise. This is His season for you. You are going through your trial because He wants to toughen you. He wants you to take hold of your land of inheritance. You will never learn to do it, though, if you continue to sit under the swaying palms. God says, "I want to make you tough for this hour."

Did you notice that the Spirit of God didn't say "hard"? He said "tough." There is a huge difference. Many Christians go through tremendous suffering, yet remain tenderhearted toward the Lord and His bride, the church.

Still, there are others who suffer life's failures and disappointments, only to become hard and hard-hearted. I watch folks in the congregation while I minister. The expressions on their faces tell me if their stomach and favorite television program are top priority.

Nothing moves them anymore. They've seen it all. Unfortunately, the process began with a simple disappointment. Slowly, their heart began to harden. They chose Meribah without even realizing it.

I sense by the Spirit of God, as I am writing these words, that this is for some of you right now as you sit reading in a hospital, airplane, propped up in a motel bed or—don't be offended—your reading room...the bathroom. You don't know if you are going forward or backward. You are not sure if you are on high ground or low ground. All you know is that something has got to break—and soon. Listen to me, my friend. "Something" is not going to break. You cannot sit around waiting for some Pentecostal magic. That is not how things happen.

YOU ARE GOING TO BREAK IT

Things are not about to change until you bring about the change by the power of God. So often we pray, "O Jesus, please break it." His reply is, "No, you break it."

Beloved, I'm not making light of your trial or what you are going through. People all over this nation and planet go through severe challenges. And often they give the devil much more credit than he deserves.

God is saying to you right now, "By commandment I will raise up My church"—that's you. However, *you* must make a decision today to be raised up above your present circumstances for your family, your children, your marriage and your church. What will your decision be?

Will you call this season "Massah"? Will you say, "God, You're making a truly godly woman (or man) out of me at last."

Every time the children of Israel came to a hard place, they wanted to go back to their last comfort station. The Spirit of God would say to you, "Oh no, this is not for going back. This time is for going on to greater things!"

GOD BRINGS US TO A PLACE OF PROVING

Our loving Father has given the pattern that the children of Israel left to us as a blueprint on how to avoid their failures. How sad it is to leave a legacy of failures, a heritage of unfulfilled destiny and unrealized dreams. No one will remember on whom or what you blamed your loss and depression.

Basically, the children of Israel did two things: They murmured and complained, and they turned against their God-given leadership. They wanted to turn back, then they turned on themselves and eventually they turned against God.

Instead of seeing the faithfulness of God and crying "Massah," they tempted and tried God's patience, saying, "Is the Lord among us or not?" (Exod. 17:7).

We do not realize the full impact of what the Israelites were saying when we read this in the English language. The question "Is the Lord among us or not?" was actually a military statement that charges an officer with desertion. Going absent without leave, or AWOL, is grounds for a court martial.

These misguided people (who were the apple of their heavenly Papa's eye) had the audacity to level a war crime charge against the only Captain who had never deserted them. I don't think God was impressed.

In essence they said, "You brought us out here, and now things are tough. Things didn't turn out the way we thought they should, and now You've abandoned us. We are not happy campers."

I can close my eyes and actually see His tears and hear His voice as once again He makes Himself answerable to His people.

"Didn't I lead you out? Didn't I bring you forth? Haven't I fed you by My hand? Is not the cloud before you and the wall of fire around you? Is not My glory here? How can you say that I have left you?"

Can you close your eyes and see His tears? Can you hear Him calling you to Himself right now? Say, "Massah, Lord." Get up and go in God's anointing.

Moses became intimidated by the circumstances. I have found that when you go through a hard place and nothing seems to work, the anointing of the Spirit of God will get you through.

Find out where the anointing is, then do whatever it takes to be around it. It will build your faith.

So, whatever happened to my son Gabriel? The doctors changed their prognosis. Six days after his emergency admission, the symptoms totally disappeared and they released him from the hospital.

God honored His Word, but He required difficult obedience on my part.

I chose Massah. Now it's your turn.

Chapter
Six

How to Know If Your
Engine Is on Fire

> *Your mother*
>
> *and father were*
>
> *passionate with*
>
> *one another*
>
> *and the result*
>
> *was ... you!*

DO YOU REMEMBER THE old sitcoms from the 1960s when Rob and Laura, Lucy and Desi and Ozzie and Harriet all slept in twin beds? That was so bizarre to me because everyone I knew who was married slept in a double bed.

When I reached puberty—and I did so with a vengeance, I might add—I decided that twin beds were totally demonic. I then realized that as couples grow older, some not only have separate beds, but also separate bedrooms.

Health problems, snoring or sleeping patterns are

often legitimate causes for couples to go their separate bedroom ways. Personally, I enjoy the warm body of my husband next to me at night.

If you are old enough to read this book, then you are mature enough to understand that you are here as a result of passion. Your mother and father were passionate with one another and the result was...you!

When a fertile couple stops having intimacy, no life can ever come forth. Likewise, when we have no intimacy with our heavenly Bridegroom, we will not produce life.

The enemy does not want you to become born again in the first place, but (I know I'm going to get letters on this one) if he can keep you passionless and infertile, his hordes will pretty much leave you alone. That is because you cease to be a threat to the kingdom of darkness.

NAVIGATING BY YOUR FEELINGS

One time I was given a wonderful opportunity to meet a retired Delta airline pilot and discuss with him my inability to understand how all those people, luggage, peanuts, screaming two-year-olds and tons of steel can stay in the air.

This gracious gentleman flew a fighter jet in the Vietnam War and retired honorably. In our meeting, he was graciously trying to connect my left-brain activity with his right-brain activity.

What he told me was quite interesting. Not all, of course, but many plane crashes are due to pilot error.

"Too much plane and too little pilot" were his words. In all the years that he had been a pilot, there was not one time when he failed to go over his checklist, whether it was a short charter flight or a long international flight. He filed a flight plan and checked with the tower as well as with his copilot and navigator. This brilliant man had followed the procedure hundreds of times, and it all was to eliminate any possible crises.

I tend to think in spiritual terms, and this time was no exception. While he was talking, I was relating everything to my relationship with my Lord.

Novice pilots have been known to fly so fast and at such incredible altitudes that they experience an inner-ear problem called vertigo. At that point they begin to rely on their feelings instead of on the instrument panel. In Cathy's "techno-terms," the little circle thingy has to line up with the little horizontal line thingy, or you won't even need to be cremated.

Many of us have done this thing so long and so many times that we think we can perform without prayer, but no one is infallible. That is why we must go through the checklist no matter how seasoned a minister we have become.

Remember, *the higher you go, the less margin for error you have.*

Unfortunately, it is easier to see the faults and failings in others than in ourselves. That is why we need a pilot, copilot and tower and ground control. All these safety mechanisms are for our protection.

God has given us His Word and His apostles,

YOU'VE GOT TO BE KIDDING,
I THOUGHT THIS WAS THE GREAT TRIBULATION!

70

prophets, pastors, teachers and evangelists. He also has placed mothers, fathers and friends in this body, all for our protection.

One of the most difficult things I have ever experienced is trying to warn a precious saint that she was beginning to rely on her feelings instead of on the instrument panel.

The apostle Paul issued a strong warning to his son in the faith, Timothy:

> This charge and admonition I commit in trust to you, Timothy, my son, in accordance with prophetic intimations which I formerly received concerning you, so that inspired and aided by them you may wage the good warfare, holding fast to faith (that leaning of the entire human personality on God in absolute trust and confidence) and having a good (clear) conscience. By rejecting and thrusting from them [their conscience], some individuals have made shipwreck of their faith.
>
> —1 TIMOTHY 1:18–19

Paul charged Timothy to remember the prophecies concerning him because there was going to be a battle.

In essence, Paul, the spiritual father, warned Timothy that warfare was coming.

Much of the ministry that God has entrusted to my husband and me is prophetic by calling. We have given prophecies to kings, presidents, lepers, housewives and doctors. God desires to speak to everyone.

I am amazed at the number of people who receive a prophetic word and then get angry and depressed when it isn't immediately fulfilled. You see, a battle wages before the victory. Some people have gotten angry with me and with others who have given them a prophetic word because they didn't understand how to rightly discern the word of the Lord.

In reading about the difference between *Visual Flight Reference* (VFR) rating and *Instrument Flight Reference* (IFR) ratings, I have found some very interesting facts:

- VFR-trained pilots can fly by visual landmarks. These, I am told, are the recreational flyers.
- IFR pilots must have additional training. They learn to fly by instruments. When they have no visual landmarks, or when the conditions are dark and stormy, they can rely on their instruments. IFR pilots are usually commercial pilots; they log many hours in their aircraft, and they can train other pilots.

I know quite a few VFR Christians. They live only by what they see. If the storm comes or the darkness descends and meets the horizon, they get in trouble. These are the *recreational* Christians. As long as they can catch the early service on Sunday morning and not have to devote too many hours for additional training, they are content.

If life contained no storms, moonless nights or

difficult situations, we could all remain "visual flight" Christians. However, that is not reality. Thus many believers "crash" and make a shipwreck of their faith.

WHY I QUIT BUYING CHEAP UNDERWEAR

I'm going to give you a *very spiritual principle,* one that is bound to offend someone, but here goes. I used to buy cheap underwear. My thinking was, If you can't see it, why bother? I had what some may call a "Renaissance" figure. Artists used to paint nude portraits of my body-type in the sixteenth century.

If you are a full-figured woman, there are certain undergarments you must buy. Men, on the other hand, have it easy. All they have to do is buy a three-to-a-pack Fruit of the Loom, size 38, and that's that.

Of course, there is an exception. If you are a sixteen-year-old boy who wears his underwear hanging out of the top of his pants (you know, with the crotch dragging on the floor), you have to buy underwear with the right design and an appropriate name on the waistband.

Women have entire departments devoted just to underwear. Full-figured women are forced to buy torturous bras called underwires. The sole purpose of underwires is to prepare you for either a labor camp or the Tribulation.

Inexpensive underwires inevitably poke out of the side seam, usually during social situations. Everyone thinks you are getting blessed, but actually you are trying to push the wire back into the bra before it perforates a main artery.

When this happens, you have three choices with the undergarment. You can: 1) throw it out, 2) try to push it back in or 3) remove the offensive wire. Let us skip to the second option, keeping in mind how spiritual this illustration is. If you try to push the wire back in, there will always be a small hole through which the offensive piece of wire will poke out later. The first time you throw the bra in the dryer, that little piece of metal will hook in a hole and make that "ka-chink-a-chink" sound as it spins around and mock you, "Aha! I'm not going back in no matter what you do to me!"

Now let's apply choice number three. We yank the whole wire out and assume that the problem is solved. Not really. When we look in the mirror, we see that we are grotesquely uneven. We wear it to church, and the next thing we know, some dear saint said she would put us on the prayer list for a financial breakthrough because it appeared that we could afford to have only one lifted.

Now stay with me, and keep in mind that this is extremely spiritual and that I am getting ready to make a point.

This all brings me back to option number one: Throw it out and go purchase good underwear. I will admit, I did not want to spend a lot of money on good underwear because the fact is . . . no one sees it.

You can only stand before your bedroom mirror for so long and tell yourself, "Oh, baby, you look terrific." Then you must get dressed and cover it all up. I told my husband that it was a shame I couldn't wear my

YOU'VE GOT TO BE KIDDING,
I THOUGHT THIS WAS THE GREAT TRIBULATION!

74

underwear on the outside of my clothes because they were so expensive. I also knew it wouldn't be long before I would be wearing mismatched underwear again.

Through all this, the Lord spoke to me. (*Yeah,* you might say.)

He said, "That in which you are willing to invest, although no one else can see it, will support you during the difficult times."

It is human nature to enjoy investing in those things that are immediately appreciated. I would rather invest in the seen rather than the unseen, but the unseen is the root that holds the tree when the storm winds blow.

DISCERNING THE PROCESS THAT LEADS TO A CRASH

What process do we unknowingly follow that leads to a crash? What I am about to share with you are certainly not all the signs of spiritual vertigo, but I have faced these situations many times over and have learned what to look for. You can call them distress signals or warning lights. If you recognize them in your life, you can immediately go to your "instruments." You can go to the Word of God, which will give you a true reading and so help you avoid a crash.

Disillusionment is the first sign to warn us that our eyes have momentarily strayed from the instruments. We give way to disappointment and begin to say things such as, "It's nothing like I thought." Remember, God is good, life is good and *all* things will work together for those...you know the oft-quoted scripture.

Our enemy is relentless in this primary tactic. This tactic is the one that has the biggest element of surprise in it. The plan is well thought-out, deliberate and meant to catch us off guard. The enemy comes to accuse us daily before God and man. He fires guilt, self-criticism and doubt. He is an expert at tearing people apart.

Satan makes sure that we see our flaws and shortcomings in order to defeat us. *If only you were a better Christian. If you just prayed more. It's November, and you are still on February 4 of your one-year Bible. What a disappointment you are to God.*

Then the enemy begins to show us the character flaws in others. He accuses over and over again. If we take our eyes off of God's love, his grip on us will tighten.

Discouragement is the next phase we encounter if we refuse to heed the warning signs of disappointment. Discouragement simply means to lose heart in people or projects that are precious to us. Signs of discouragement are feelings of being totally alone, frustration and mounting guilt. We all get to that place from time to time. We must learn "IFR," instrument training.

In Psalm 63, David recounts again how he had to learn the secret of the presence of the Lord. When all of David's men spoke of stoning him, David, feeling totally alone, went to his God for counsel. (See 1 Samuel 30.) "Pursue, overtake and recover all" was

You've Got to Be Kidding,
I Thought This Was the Great Tribulation!

76

God's answer.

God makes allowances for those horrible attacks—He has given us a way of escape.

I know what it is like to have someone say she would love me forever. It wasn't long before I was a disappointment to this person, and she told me so. I felt wounded and betrayed because it was a friend whom I held in high esteem. I assumed her accusations to be true. For days and weeks I labored under the guilt that I had been a disappointment to her.

Even though all the right words were spoken, I had a huge, gaping wound. If what she had said was true, I was not capable of ministry. She said that she could find no sin in me, but that I had changed.

Still suffering from the loss of my father, the enemy took advantage of a situation to discourage me even more. I started to nosedive, and I felt as if I could never pull out of it.

Every believer will experience persecutions and trials in life that he or she feels unable to bear. I had no one with whom I could share my heartache, except my husband, because I would not dishonor my friend. If she was right, then I deserved it.

Do you see the plan of the enemy? After he discourages you, he will then try to discredit you.

Several weeks after this altercation, I was sitting alone in my car in the parking lot of a church where I had just ministered. The meeting had not seemed like much of a success, and I was feeling miserable.

My thoughts were interrupted by a gentle rapping on the car window. A man stood outside. Lowering the window, I asked if I could help him. The man began to weep and said sweetly, "Those words that were spoken over you and about you...The Lord told me to tell you that the letter was not from Him and that the words were not from heaven." Then he walked away.

No one knew that the rebuke had come by letter. I was in a strange city, sitting in my car in the church parking lot. I was not looking for vindication, but my wonderful, loving God sent His servant to help me out of discouragement. He didn't do it publicly, but privately...just for me!

My friend, those are the times when character is built. Just as for David in Ziklag, when the city was burned to the ground, the spoil stolen and families kidnapped, your best friend says to you, "Aha, I knew it. You're cursed, and you are going to start growing black facial hair." That's pretty bad.

To not pull out of discouragement is to open the door to *depression*. Such depression will manifest itself as listlessness, a lack of enthusiasm for life, little drive for fighting the devil and multiple physical problems.

We all have a "blue" day once in a while, but depression is becoming too common among Christians today.

If you deal with depression, try fasting television, newspapers and magazines. Give your thoughts, heart and attitude to the Lord. Bug your pastor until he either helps you (or medicates you). If you are the pastor, don't be afraid to ask for help.

The children of Israel lived in this emotional state

before they bought the big one: *despair.* They had no hope or faith in God in spite of all He had done for them.

Many live in despair because it saves them from more disappointment. If they don't get their hopes up, they won't be disappointed.

What a horrible place to live. Christians who live in despair become bitter, sarcastic and hypercritical. They criticize every ministry on television from their comfortable seat on the couch. All their fellowship is based around their problems.

You may be wondering, *But what do I do? Where do I go?* Please know that you are not alone. No matter how far you have gone or how long it has been, the Master's arms are open to scoop you up and love on you.

Never give up! You will reap in due season. Keep your eyes on the instruments, because I don't think there is a parachute on board!

Chapter
Seven

Victim, Vacuum or Victor?

> *When we stomp our foot and demand our own way, that's sin—the sin of selfishness.*

LET NOTHING BE DONE through selfish ambition or conceit, but in lowliness of mind let each esteem others better than himself. Let each of you look out not only for his own interests, but also for the interests of others.

—**PHILIPPIANS 2:3–4**, NKJV

The truth is, some people just seem to be plagued by the thing they hate the most...a recurrent sin problem that enslaves them. No matter what they do, what they say or who they hear preach, it just dogs them. They've stood in every prayer line and gone through all kinds of deliverance; they've come to the point of being too embarrassed to let any of their Christian friends know they're still having a sin problem.

They seem victimized by sin, and they often complain of feeling like victims. They just can't help it, so they believe they must learn to live with that little sin problem. This is what's called "victim thinking," and it's a choice. You can choose to accept things just the way they are and stay shackled to that little sin problem, or you can make some changes that will result in your maturing and becoming a victor in Christ.

That little sin problem, after all, is nothing new. Sin has been around since the fall of Adam, and it's our old, uncrucified Adamic nature that's the problem, not the sin. When flesh rules, sin results. When we stomp our foot and demand our own way, that's sin— the sin of selfishness. It's the place where I believe we start to wander out of the way.

Four little words from a sentence in Philippians define and characterize this sin problem: "Do nothing from selfishness" (Phil. 2:3, NAS).

Now, selfishness is also nothing new. What we're seeing manifest in the church today is nothing new. And it's not limited to the laity either. Paul described some of the church leaders of his day in Philippians 2:21: "For all seek their own, not the things which are of Christ Jesus" (NKJV).

Where did this selfishness—this "sin attitude"—start? It started at Genesis 3:6:

> So when the woman saw that the tree was good
> for food, that it was pleasant to the eyes, and a

tree desirable to make one wise, she took of its fruit and ate. She also gave to her husband with her, and he ate.

—NKJV

With that single act of disobedience—that seemingly small and insignificant act—a frightening thing entered into that peaceful garden, and mankind became afflicted with something known as *original sin.*

The biblical definition of *original sin* is connected to Genesis 3:6. Until sin entered into human experience when Adam and Eve ate the forbidden fruit of the tree of the knowledge of good and evil, man was guileless, guiltless and without sin. Eve violated the direct command of God by eating the fruit. But when Adam, the head of the human race, followed her into that sin, his sin affected all future generations. Thus Adam passed to all mankind a corrupt nature. That means all the sin we commit today is a result of that perverted inheritance.

Here's how Paul explained that corrupt nature of ours in Romans:

> Therefore, just as through one man sin entered the world, and death through sin, and thus death spread to all men, because all sinned—(For until the law sin was in the world, but sin is not imputed when there is no law. Nevertheless death reigned from Adam to Moses, even over those who had not sinned according to the likeness of the transgression of Adam, who is a type

of Him who was to come.

But the free gift is not like the offense. For if by the one man's offense many died, much more the grace of God and the gift by the grace of the one Man, Jesus Christ, abounded to many. And the gift is not like that which came through the one who sinned. For the judgment which came from one offense resulted in condemnation, but the free gift which came from many offenses resulted in justification. For if by the one man's offense death reigned through the one, much more those who receive abundance of grace and of the gift of righteousness will reign in life through the One, Jesus Christ.)

Therefore, as through one man's offense judgment came to all men, resulting in condemnation, even so through one Man's righteous act the free gift came to all men, resulting in justification of life. For as by one man's disobedience many were made sinners, so also by one Man's obedience many will be made righteous. Moreover the law entered that the offense might abound. But where sin abounded, grace abounded much more, so that as sin reigned in death, even so grace might reign through righteousness to eternal life through Jesus Christ our Lord.

—Romans 5:12–21, NKJV

We still inherit that corrupt nature, but when we become Christians, we have access to Christ's righteousness. As long as we stay in our old, Adamic ways, we won't be able to appropriate that Christlikeness. Yet it's right there, beckoning—the antidote to that little "sin problem." We have a new inheritance, but we must learn how to walk in that inheritance. In order to do that, we must stop walking in the old ways, the ways of the flesh.

THE CENTER OF THE UNIVERSE

One day when Randi and I were talking, our daughter Jerusha, who was just two at the time, ran over to us and grabbed us both. One pudgy little hand grabbed my hand and the other grabbed for Randi's as she declared her need for our immediate attention.

She had grown accustomed to being the center of our universe. She liked being that. Now she was afraid of being edged out because she saw how absorbed in conversation Randi and I were, and she realized that she was not being included. So we began to deal with that. Soon the truth began to dawn that, although her father and I loved her very, very much, Jerusha was not the center of the entire universe... just ours!

Sin entered the Garden when man began to desire to be the center of the entire universe. When he started to want to be seen, known and recognized, he started down the slippery slope that eventually led to the loss of his eternal inheritance.

He wanted it all, and instead he lost it all.

He had it all, and he wanted to keep it.

Poor Jerusha! She seems to be the one I'm using in

this chapter to provide all my examples. (I'm going to have to take her to the mall or something after I've finished this book in order to make up for using her so often as my "example"!) Another time when Jerusha was small, her daddy took her out to buy her an ice cream cone. As the ice cream began to melt faster than she could eat it, her daddy asked her for a bite.

"No!" she cried, snatching the ice cream cone away from his reach.

And that was that. She came home covered in chocolate goo, and her daddy never did get a bite. I thought about that episode over the years, and I began to see a correlation between Jerusha's selfish decision and the way we, the church, have a habit of acting selfishly. Jerusha's daddy had given her a gift: a chocolate ice cream cone. Selfishly, she wanted to keep it all for herself, even though most of it melted and wound up dripping all over her dress. Like Jerusha, we've been given gifts. Yet we don't want to share. We want to keep all those gifts and even get some more. Selfishly, we want to *have*, not *give*. We want to be acquirers, not givers.

The day that dawned on me, I realized that one mark of Christian maturity is becoming a giver, not remaining an acquirer. That's going to cost something. It's going to mean putting away the childish things. (See 1 Corinthians 13:11.)

Trust me, when you start doing that, it's going to hurt because some flesh will have to die.

"GOD LOVES ME JUST THE WAY I AM!"

When Randi and I married, I was twenty-one. I had been raised in the church and had walked with Jesus all my life. My dear father was a pastor, and I thought I was very mature and seasoned. Yet I married a man who seemed convinced that I was childish, immature and in need of correction for my various childish decisions and selfish attitudes.

"You're too demanding!" I'd respond. "Jesus loves me just the way I am!"

Even my family agreed. "He's too hard on you, honey," they commiserated. "Randi just expects too much."

Then came the day when the Holy Spirit convicted me that my husband had been right after all. Through his training and commitment to be the high priest of our family, Randi's influence began to forge in me endurance and strength, out of which eventually came a ministry. When God discovered that He could entrust me to others, He began to entrust me *with* others.

But I had to do some changing, and first I had to put away childish things. I had to stop being a taker, an acquirer...and learn to give.

Ouch!

BLACK HOLES IN THE BODY OF CHRIST

A black hole is a hypothetical body in space, a place—supposedly invisible—where matter folds into itself instead of expanding outward. Astronomers believe

You've Got to Be Kidding,
I Thought This Was the Great Tribulation!

90

these black holes to be collapsed stars, once bright, but now burned out and so dense that neither light nor matter can escape its gravitational field. These black holes virtually eat up space, a little like Pac Man, only more serious.

Astronomers estimate that if Earth's sun ever became a black hole, it would be four miles in diameter. But if our sun ever became a black hole, we'd all be dead. So much for that theory!

Black holes... even light can't emanate from them. Scientists can't figure out how black holes function because anything that gets too near gets sucked in. And disappears.

Sin operates just like one of those black holes. When we get too near, it sucks us in and pulls us into a darkness so dense that no light escapes.

And sin can usually be reduced to these two words: *illegal desire.*

Whatever else sin did to you and me, it created in us a black hole... a place that takes and then drains and sucks the life and light out of everything that dares to go near it. It creates in you and me a "selfish phenomenon," an inner vacuum that just sucks everything down into itself and reduces us to wanting just one thing: to acquire.

Illegal desire makes us want to acquire.

Whatever the various phenomena connected with sin, one thing is for sure: It turned us into acquirers. Some of us have become mature acquirers, granted, but that just means we've become "mature black holes." We want to remain the center of the universe and have everything brought to us, done for us and tailored to us. We want others to cater to our every whim. We want to be loved, revered, appreciated and showered with praise and presents.

After we get it, we want to keep it all and go right back out to acquire some more. "More is never enough," as Miss Piggy seems so fond of reminding us.

EMOTIONAL BLACK HOLES

Some people are not simply "black holes" when it comes to acquiring things; they're emotional black holes who can't ever seem to be filled. They can't get enough affirmation, esteem, affection or security to really trust someone else. So divorce appears to be the only option. Divorce often happens when two "black holes"—two acquirers—marry one another. Neither has learned how to give, and neither has any intention of learning how.

She claws at him, demanding, "Meet my needs! Meet my needs!"

He claws at her: "Meet my needs! Meet my needs!"

They claw at each other until they can't stand it anymore and get a divorce. Now they have two new partners to claw apart, demanding, "Meet my needs! Meet my needs!"

Today's church is teeming with those who demand, "Meet my needs! Meet my needs! Bless me! Pray for me! Visit me! Strengthen me! Show me! Teach me! Help me!" They're habitual takers who view themselves as victims of life's hard knocks. No amount of care-giving and concern will solve their problems or fill the black holes in their souls. They have learned that codependency works. Well, sort of ...

INTELLECTUAL BLACK HOLES

Then there are the intellectual black holes. These individuals want knowledge simply for its own sake. They're the "know everythings" among us, those whose "head knowledge" of spiritual things endeavors to make up for the lack of "heart knowledge." Thousands of Christians fall into this category, sad to say.

These individuals are ever learning, yet never able to come to the knowledge of the truth. They move around, ears tickling, from place to place, adding to their vast storehouses of knowledge. Yet, they can't find time to sit down for an intimate moment with Jesus. He warned us that there would be those who claimed to know Him, yet were not known by Him.

It is possible for us all to know Him, just as it's possible for us all to receive that antidote to sin. The only way out of all those black holes that sin has created in us is to take on the new nature of Christ. He purchased it for us on the cross at Calvary, and it is part of our inheritance package if we will just receive it. "He died for all, that those who live should live no longer for themselves, but for Him who died for them and rose again" (2 Cor. 5:15, NKJV).

Because that inheritance is exactly the same for

every believer who will reach out and appropriate it, no one has any excuse to continue on, victimlike, in the flesh. Now, you and I both know that we cannot jump from living according to the flesh to walking in the Spirit with one snap of our fingers. A single decision is not enough to complete that transaction. But the decision to walk in the Spirit—as a victor and not as a victim—is where it starts. Jesus died for us so He could impart to us His new nature. As we press on in Him toward wholeness—acknowledging that there must be a healing of the thing in us that sucks everything up into its vortex—He will do the work in us, and the reverse will happen. Instead of being a vacuum, where the people and things we acquire fall in never to be seen or heard from again, we'll be mature, giving, living examples of the light of Christ.

If we'll just ask Him, Jesus will redesign us into givers, not takers, changing us from victims to victors. He'll fill the vacuum within and transform us from black holes to bright lights for Christ.

The basic change, however, comes when we are transformed from living for self into living for Him in all spheres of life—mentally, physically, financially and intellectually. When we allow Him to change us, we cast off the various iniquities that are connected to original sin and passed down to us from generation to generation. Then we acquire some new, eternal qualities.

- *We acquire God's forgiveness.* When we learn to give it out, we receive it. Refusing to forgive makes a person a spiritual black hole. Forgiving others means receiving forgiveness when we most need it and least deserve it.

- *We acquire God's love.* None of us are worthy of God's love. It's a gift, and when we love others—even the unlovely—we receive a generous portion back. However, do not confuse loving others with approval. God loves the world. He loves sinners. But He neither loves nor approves of their sin.

- *We acquire God's gifts.* He will gift us with spiritual gifts and the fruit of the Spirit, but not so we can keep them. He wants us to become conduits of His love and empowerment. He gives us gifts so that we, in turn, give them out again.

- *We acquire God's healing.* Black holes are never just "healed." They keep taking and taking and never get healing. In order for a black hole to become healed, he or she must learn to give. Giving is the only path to healing.

- *We acquire covenant prosperity.* This one's tricky, because God's purpose for such abundant blessing is to reach the nations. The prosperity message is great, as long as it does not become a black hole to you. God wants to bless and prosper His people because we can't be a blessing unless we're blessed. When we are blessed, the key to avoid becoming a black hole is simple: We must give so God can pour His blessing through us to a world in desperate need of His blessing.

You see, there are some things worth acquiring after all! I'll take two of each, please!

Chapter
Eight

Did You Know
God Loves a Nobody?

> *I was still in my sweats, scheming how I could make my way to the airport and fly home before I was missed.*

LYING ON THE MOTEL ROOM bed, I kept leafing through the conference brochure. Instead of being ecstatic, thrilled and overjoyed, I had a growing feeling of panic in the pit of my stomach.

Here I was in a city I love—Sydney, Australia—at one of the greatest churches on the planet, invited to be a speaker at their Hillsong '99 Conference. From the time I arrived I was told that I was the first woman ever to be invited to a "Hills" conference as a speaker and that mine was the first prophetic ministry to participate. I was to be the first speaker, the first night . . . opening night.

They were excited, but the more they talked, the sicker I became ... until I thought I was going to throw up right there and then. I knew this conference would be a life-changing event that would impact nations for generations. And to think that I was to be a part of this wondrous visitation from God! That was the problem ... which was not just a problem; it was my problem. You see, the longer I looked at the program with its list of distinguished speakers, the more intimidated I became.

Looking from one photograph to another, it was easy to understand why *they* were invited to minister. What I didn't understand was why *I* was there. The more I read and reread the schedule, the sicker I became.

Thirty minutes before my ride was to arrive to take me to the meeting, I was still in my sweats, scheming how I could make my way to the airport and fly home before I was missed. Of course, I would have to pay for my own airline ticket, which meant I'd have to take a second job at McDonald's for the next forty years.

At that precise moment my cell phone rang. Much to my surprise and relief it was my husband, Randi. His first words were, "What's wrong?" It was 12:30 A.M. in Florida, and the Lord had told him to call me. At $3 a minute, he listened to me as I poured out my heart, telling him that I was a lowly worm and didn't deserve to be there. They had surely made a mistake, and I was ready to come home. When I got done wailing, he asked, "Are you finished?" "Yes," I sobbed.

He took a deep breath, and I will never, ever forget what he said to me. "You are right, honey. In comparison to all those wonderful speakers, you are a nobody." At that point, I wondered if he had heard what I had just told him, because what he said was definitely not a blessing.

I was thankful that he continued by saying, "Honey, did you hear me? You are a nobody, *but you are not a nothing.* You are nobody, sent by Someone, to do something for someone at that conference. God did not make a mistake."

The power of that revelation broke the spirit of fear and intimidation off of me instantly. Randi was right. I was a nobody, but I wasn't a nothing. I had a word from heaven for God's people. All He asked was that this nobody be His faithful representative.

NOT A NOTHING

There is a passage of scripture that talks about a man whose entire life consisted of trials. Second Kings 6:8–10 says this:

> When the king of Syria was warring against Israel, after counseling with his servants, he said, In such and such a place shall be my camp. Then the man of God sent to the king of Israel, saying, Beware that you pass not such a place, for the Syrians are coming down there. Then the king of Israel sent to the place of which [Elisha] told and warned him; and thus he protected and saved

himself there repeatedly. Therefore the mind of the king of Syria was greatly troubled by this thing. He called his servants and said, Will you show me who of us is for the king of Israel?

It was so awesome! The king of Syria was after Israel all the time, but Elisha would get a word of knowledge and then tell the king of Israel what God was speaking to him about how to avoid the enemy. Finally the king of Syria decided that there had to be a spy in his camp, and he tried to find out who this spy was. One of his servants told him that it was not one of his own who was betraying him; it was the prophet Elisha. "[He] tells the king of Israel the words that you speak in your bedchamber" (2 Kings 6:12).

There is nothing secret from God. The "bedchamber" represents your private domain, the place that is your sanctuary. The enemy king knew the reputation of the prophet Elisha, but this is how he responded: "Go and see where he is, that I may send and seize him" (2 Kings 6:13). Now that is really funny to me. Elisha knows every move the king makes, and now the king of Syria thinks he can sneak one by?

Neither can the devil sneak anything by God. Nothing can come to you unless your loving Father has first given His yes or no to it. That's why you don't have to hit the panic button and cry, "O God, what's going on?" You can say, "Father, I thank You. I can trust You. You are faithful. You knew this was going to happen, and nothing's changed."

The king of Syria sent horses and chariots and surrounded the city by night. Think of it...an army of soldiers, horses and chariots were dispatched for one middle-aged, balding prophet who probably couldn't run very fast (no doubt because he went out to Denny's every night after the service). All this was for one man.

How dangerous are you to the kingdom of darkness? How many does the enemy have to send after you? Perhaps all he needs is one little demon to cause your husband to yell at you, and you back down and run. You see, the higher you go in God and the more dangerous you are to the kingdom of darkness, the more the enemy will send after you.

I believe the greatest lie perpetrated against the body of Christ is this: Satan is alive and well and living on planet earth. You say, "But the Word says that we wrestle not against flesh and blood...we know the devil is out there." The Word also tells us that when Jesus was on the cross He said, "It is finished!" What was finished? The battle was over. Jesus went down into hell, took the keys and stripped the enemy. We have the power to put Satan under our feet.

It's like the Japanese soldier who crash-landed in the jungle and, unaware that the war was over, kept fighting long after the treaty was signed. That is a picture of what the kingdom of darkness is like. There are still some demons out there who don't realize the war is over. They don't know that Jesus signed the contract in His own blood. He did the hard part; all you have to do is kick the enemy and take the spoils. Some of us act as though we aren't aware the battle is over, either. We scream and scream at the devil, binding and loosing, but *it is finished.* There comes a time when we need to begin to praise and worship.

The Syrians came after the prophet Elisha. When his servant arose the next morning and saw that the city was surrounded, he probably wondered, *How will we ever win the battle?* Have you ever gone to bed one night with everything going great, only to wake up the next morning and find out the devil had pooped all over your front yard? *What happened? Yesterday was so wonderfully great!*

Elisha did not jump out of bed and suggest that they have a prayer meeting to pull down strongholds. He just looked at his servant. He was more concerned about the one he was mentoring than he was about the enemy. When you live your life so those around you see your faith, you become a living testament and witness to the power, faith and glory of God. Your lifestyle takes the place of ten Bible studies.

Elisha had already sold out to God. He did not panic. He looked directly at his servant and said, "Lord, I pray that You open his eyes that he may see that there are more with us than there are with the enemy." (See 2 Kings 6:16-17.)

That is my prayer for you...that you may see that you are not a nothing. There are more with you than there are with the enemy. God is backing you up 100 percent in heaven, saying *yes* and *amen* concerning you.

HAVE YOU GOT ANY ENEMIES?

God is faithful. Second Kings 6:23–25 says, "So [the king] prepared great provision for them, and when they had eaten and drunk, he sent them away, and they went to their master. And the bands of Syria came no more into the land of Israel. Afterward, Ben-hadad king of Syria gathered his whole army and went up and besieged Samaria. And a great famine came to Samaria. ..." The passage goes on to tell us that they were selling donkey heads and doves' dung for an outrageous sum. (Yuk!)

A woman cried out to the king of Israel for help. He answered by telling her that if the Lord didn't help her, how could he? He was being sarcastic. He had no faith. He believed that God was doing this to them. His attitude was, *If God is doing this, how can I help?* He wasn't greater than God.

That's always been the mistake through the ages. Job made that mistake, too. "Though He slay me, yet will I trust Him" (Job 13:15, NKJV). He was in deception when he said that. God does not go around slaying His servants; it is the enemy who does that. God's desire for Job was that he would have more in the end than he had in the beginning. We love to quote that scripture out of some perverted thought that *we* will be faithful even if *He* tortures and then kills us. How ludicrous. That is not the God I serve.

The king asked the woman, "What ails you?" She told him the story of how they were so hungry that she and another woman made an agreement to kill and eat one woman's son one day and the other woman's the next. You know the story . . . they ate one son, and when it the other woman's turn to give up her baby, she reneged. When the king heard this, he rent his clothes and wore sackcloth. He said, "May God do so to me, and more also, if the head of Elisha son of Shaphat shall stand on him this day!" (2 Kings 6:28–31).

Now here is Elisha, the man who saved the backside of the king of Israel over and over again by giving him prophetic words about the plans of the enemy. Elisha went out of his way to give the king words from heaven. Suddenly, when the king doesn't understand what is happening, he is ready to kill the prophet.

Be careful whom you make your enemy. There are times when God uses certain people to speak into our lives. Then the time comes when we don't like what they said or we don't agree with them, and immediately we turn on them.

The king of Israel blamed Elisha and went after him. After all the prophet had done for him, this is how the king repaid him when he came to a hard place. People always tend to want to turn against the leadership, the boss or the pastor. Are your leaders perfect? Of course not. If they are God's anointed servants, however, we are to leave them alone.

FROM FAMINE TO FEAST

The story continues. Elisha sat in his house, along with the elders, and the king sent a man to behead

Elisha. Before the messenger arrived, Elisha said to the elders, "See how this son of Jezebel, a murderer, is sending to remove my head? When he gets here, bar the door against him because we are going to wait until the power behind him gets here." The king didn't want to dirty his hands; he sent someone else ahead of him to do the dirty work. While Elisha was talking, the messenger came to him. The king was right behind him. When the king saw Elisha alive, he said, "This evil is from the Lord. Why should I wait any longer and expect Him to withdraw His punishment? What, Elisha, can be done now?" Elisha just looked at him and said, "Hear the word of the Lord. Thus says the Lord ..." (See 2 Kings 6:32–7:1)

You have heard me say many times that when you are going through a difficult time, dig out the word you received from the Lord. Many times when we get a word we think that we understand and know what it means. God gives us a word because He knows that we are about to enter a famine and that we need the word to war with when we are in the middle of that crisis.

"Tomorrow about this time a measure of fine flour will sell for a shekel and two measures of barley for a shekel in the gate of Samaria" (2 Kings 7:1). How fast can God turn a famine into a feast? He doesn't need twenty-four hours. Actually, in this instance He took His time. He told Elisha that in twenty-four hours the famine would turn into a feast.

You may be going through a famine right now. At this writing, Randi and I are experiencing the "summer slump" in finances that a lot of churches go through, except we are not salaried. His cough turned into pneumonia, and we have two conferences coming up. We had to get to the place where we battled the devil and told him, "You will not discredit the Word of the Lord. We know your plot and scheme, and we are going to keep on going." Your famine may be physical or financial, or you may simply be in a place where you question God. I say to you, "Thus saith the Lord, 'I can turn your famine around within twenty-four hours.'"

Now, the captain on whose hand the king leaned... no, wait, let me first make a comparison. Elisha's servant said, "We're going to die!" But because Elisha was mentoring him, he let the servant know that there were more on their side than on the enemy's. The king's son in the faith, the captain, said with sarcasm (which he got from hanging around the king), "If God were to open up windows in heaven and pour the barley out, how could this thing ever be?" He was full of doubt and unbelief. Elisha looked at this captain and said, "You'll see it, but you won't partake of it." (See 2 Kings 7:2.)

One day as I was driving by myself to a meeting, God spoke to me and said, "Tell My people that no longer will I bless the messenger just for the sake of the message." I asked God what He meant. He told me that many have had a great message and preached the Word of the Lord, but their lives were a mess. They did not walk in holiness or integrity. Their personal lives were a mess, yet they continued to preach the Word. "I honored them because of the message.

But no longer will I honor the messenger for the sake of the message." All you have to do is drive to Fort Mill, the former site of PTL, and you'll know what He meant. Buildings are nothing to God. It became a conference center, then it sold again and the new owners put in a bar and country club. What is blessed can't be cursed, so that didn't work.

I told the Lord, "I knew principally why You won't bless the messenger anymore, but what are You telling me?" I pulled off to the side of the interstate, weeping, and the Lord answered me: "Cathy, the reason that I don't have to bless the messenger for the sake of the message anymore is because there are too many people in the wings waiting to take your place. Many people out there are praying, serving, carrying cups of water, getting to the church early to make sure everything is OK, and staying late to clean up. If you won't obey Me, that's fine, but there are too many people out there waiting and willing to pay the price, and I will bring them in."

These nobodies are just waiting for the chance to be used by God. In the past we've had great men and women whom God raised up, but this new generation has never even heard of them. Why? God began using a whole new group of people to take the place of those who failed.

NOBODIES HAVE NOTHING TO LOSE

Elisha told the captain, who was the king's right-hand man, "You'll see it, but you'll not eat of it." This is important. God uses His servants to speak a word into our lives, yes. But in the past we have thought it was the preacher's job to preach the Word while we all sat there and took the offering. Then we sat for fifteen more hours while everyone went through the prayer line. When we all went home to have dinner, the pastor was still there praying for everyone. We wanted him available to stand with us and pray for us, and we complained because he didn't call or visit us when we were sick.

The Lord says we've got it totally wrong. That's not the job of the pastor or prophet. They are there to train and equip the saints for the work of the ministry. The old theory of allowing the guest speaker to do all the work was never God's will. That's why we have superstars in the body of Christ. Everyone wants to receive, but few want to really obey God. God is saying, "I use the prophet to deliver the word, but now I must look for a vehicle to bring the miracle to pass."

The very next verse in this passage says, "Now four men who were lepers..." (2 Kings 7:3). I love that. God had to really go down the ladder to find someone willing to obey Him and be used to bring a miracle in fulfillment of the word. He doesn't tell us that the man or woman of God will prophesy and then go out and fight the battle or come to your house and pet your devil on the head.

I have been in meetings where those who sit in the back of the church filled the backseats. These people do not come up when you call for those who need prayer. They want special attention. They wait until the service is over and the anointing has lifted, and then they will say, "I know I should have come up, but I am going through this awful thing and I need 'special' prayer." No, they don't. They just needed to be obedient and go up with everyone else. What good will it do them if the anointing has lifted?

In 2 Kings 7 God looked for someone who had nothing to gain. He found four men who were eaten away with a disease, socially unacceptable, cast out and unwanted. Sitting outside the gate, they decided that since they weren't doing anything anyway—except waiting to die—they had nothing to lose. God is looking for people who have nothing to lose.

When the four lepers dragged themselves out, God saw their faith. The prophet prophesied it, and then God looked for a vehicle to bring the word to pass. God took His mighty microphone, placed it at the lepers' feet, then ran it through the amplifier of heaven and caused it to come out through the camp of the Assyrians. The soldiers didn't hear the sound of four lepers crawling through the grass. What they heard was the sound of armies coming after them.

Suddenly, the enemy dropped everything and ran. They left everything behind...then enter the lepers! The place was empty. They had a wonderful time enjoying the spoils. You ask, "What's the point?" Those who are willing to cross over first get the first of the spoils. Those who are willing to take God at His Word, those who have nothing to lose and who are willing to give, sow and speak, are the first ones to enjoy the blessing.

YOU'VE GOT TO BE KIDDING,
I THOUGHT THIS WAS THE GREAT TRIBULATION!

112

One time I prophesied to a couple at a meeting something I had never said before. The word of the Lord was that "they had stood and stood against Goliath, but Goliath is getting ready to go down, and when he does, you get his lunch." I imagine it was a huge lunch. When you take Goliath—when you take your giant—you step into what has already been appropriated for you, and you get his lunch. Your situation may seem difficult right now, but when God turns it around, the glory of God comes. If you know anyone who has ever been blessed and rewarded, and whose life shows visible signs of God's moving and of His blessings, you can know for sure that they had to pay a price. I don't resent anything good that men and women of God receive because most of them deserve it. They have paid a price.

The lepers decided that they had better tell someone about what they had stumbled into. They were probably sitting there like the pirates of the Caribbean (with jeweled necklaces and medallions around their necks and barbecue sauce all over their faces). So they went and told the king of Israel. When the king heard their news, he turned to his servant, the captain, and told him to do crowd control. "Stand at the gate as the people come in when we announce that the famine is over."

In 2 Kings 7:17, the captain was trampled as the people came in to get the food. He died just as the man of God had foretold when this servant of the king made fun of the prophecy. It was twenty-four hours later when he saw it but didn't partake of it.

That's what doubt, unbelief and negative words will do in your life. They will cause you to see the blessing, but you will never partake of it.

Just as God turned the famine around in twenty-four hours, so the man, the captain who was next to the king, died as Elisha had prophesied. God can pull down governments, and He can set them up. He can take lawsuits that have been planned against you; He can preserve your job when you thought you were laid off. He can do anything He desires in order to bless you.

He will do what He said He will do. Are you willing to say, "I have nothing to lose. If we sit here, we will die. If we go in, we will die. But I would rather die doing something than die doing nothing"?

Chapter
Nine

Taking Your Family Into
God's Favor When They
Don't Really Want to Go

> *For people like
> me, the phrase
> "make it plain"
> is not just for
> shouting back
> as the minister
> preaches.*

ONE EVENING DURING A **church service a man of God called me out of the crowd and prophesied these words over me:**

"Daughter, the Lord says that you are simple...."

The word of the Lord continued, but I got the giggles. It was not "Holy Ghost manifested laughter"; it just struck me as funny. Here in our country *simple* is used at times to describe a person of diminished mental capacity. My giggles soon turned into extremely loud belly laughs, then snorts. All this was out loud, on the platform and into the microphone. If there ever was a manifestation of the prophetic word, this was it.

All the spiritual people thought that I was getting blessed, but all my friends knew better. I knew what the man of God meant, and I knew what the Holy Spirit was saying. Actually, you could say it was a compliment.

The gospel in and of itself *is* simple. The more we complicate it, the more lost we become. Many of the comments I receive about my books are that people are grateful for the simplicity in the writing.

I realize this isn't for everyone. Some Christians have a Greek-Hebrew-eschatology deficiency. They want to walk where Jesus walked; dance the prophetic, interpretive dance of Watchman Nee (you can envision Watchman Nee dancing with streamers and tambourines, can't you?); and experience an intellectual thrill.

Sorry, I'm just not that smart. For people like me, the phrase "make it plain" is not just for shouting back as the minister preaches. Simple people literally need you to "make it plain." So with that thought in mind, the Holy Spirit wants to really encourage those of you who are going through a trial by fire with your family.

GOD'S FORMULA FOR FAVOR

Therefore has the Lord recompensed me according to my righteousness (my uprightness and right standing with Him), according to the cleanness of my hands in His sight. With the kind and merciful You will show Yourself kind and merciful, with an upright man You will show

Yourself upright, with the pure You will show
Yourself pure, and with the perverse You will
show Yourself contrary.
—PSALM 18:24–26

What a lovely, simple principle we see here. The
way you respond to God is the way He will respond to
you. How we respond to God affects our destiny.

In the Book of 2 Samuel, the seventh chapter, something happened in David's life that profoundly
affected him and his family forever. We find David
finally living a successful, prosperous life. He is really
living well, but he is grieving because the Lord, or
"His glory," the Ark of the Covenant, is outside under
a tent—and that just doesn't seem right.

The king lives in a palace, but God's magnificent
glory is outside in a canvas tent. David then makes a
simple decision: "I want to build God a house." He
begins to make preparations in his heart and mind,
but then God stops him.

We read that David is forbidden to build God's
house, but that God will give him a son, and this son
will build the house. Even though David was not
allowed to build the temple, we all know that David's
desire moved God's heart in a way that we cannot
even imagine.

We learn to know others by spending time with
them. My husband and I had known each other for
only six weeks before we were married, so needless to
say, there was a whole lot we did not know about
each other.

The week of our honeymoon was coming to an end. We were in a cabin in the mountains, almost destitute, when my sweetheart happily announced that he was going to prepare dinner for me that evening. Nervously I handed over the last of our wedding-gift money and watched him drive off to the grocery store. Two hours, three grocery bags and eleven cents later, he returned.

Because he wanted this meal to be a complete surprise, Randi asked that I stay in the bedroom until all the preparations were finished and he could totally surprise and impress me. I tried to distract myself from the banging and clanging of the pots.

About midway through this ordeal, partly out of curiosity and boredom, and partly because I needed a potty break, I quietly slipped out of the bedroom. I couldn't help but peek around the corner, down the hall, up some stairs and into the living room. There, hunched over a blazing fire in the fireplace, was my brand-new husband with a pair of tongs, fishing out pieces of chicken that had fallen through the grate and into the fire. He shook some ash off the meat and proceeded to place it all back on the grate to continue cooking. Holding my hand over my mouth to stifle a scream, I ran back to the bedroom.

Up until that time, my idea of healthy food was a box of blueberry Pop-Tarts.

The hour of truth arrived, and Randi led me to my chair. There on the table were place settings for two, including fresh cut flowers, all bathed in candlelight. Soft music played in the background. Then he served the feast he had prepared . . . a large piece of blackened chicken, followed by two heaping spoonfuls of Brussels sprouts and approximately four cups of almost cooked brown rice.

I hate chicken (unless it's in a salad). When I cut into my charred piece of chicken, the inside bled dark pink juice all over the plate. Not done . . . not good! Also, I have a personal belief that Brussels sprouts is the vegetable from hell. It is the gagging vegetable— little heads that roll around in your mouth.

Being a Southern girl, there is only one kind of rice, and that is white rice covered with thick brown pan gravy. You know, it's the kind of gravy that, upon consumption, causes immediate heart failure. We never ate brown rice, let alone dry, with no taste, no flavor and no butter. And my beverage that night was a choice of bottled water with lemon or unsweetened iced tea.

Dear God! It was a plot! Being a preacher's kid, I learned a long time ago the art of pushing my food around on the plate without actually ever having to eat any of it. It didn't take my sweetheart very long to see that I had hidden pieces of chicken (that only hours before had been having a loving chicken conversation with her sisters) underneath hunks of little Brussels heads and hard, thick-as-plank grains of rice.

I was caught! He was crushed as I tactfully explained that these were my three most hated food groups. His eyes filled with tears as his face, which up to that point was innocent and without guile, showed signs of the hurt my words had caused him.

YOU'VE GOT TO BE KIDDING,
I THOUGHT THIS WAS THE GREAT TRIBULATION!

122

"I'm sorry, Cathy. I was only trying to bless you." Immediately I shot back with, "If you want to bless me, you should first find out what I like." I can now say that what I lacked in wisdom, I equally lacked in sensitivity!

During my prayer time the next day, the Holy Spirit spoke to me and said, "Daughter, if you love Me, why don't you find out what it is that *I* like?"

We can offer God the best of what we like, but if it is not what He has asked for, it becomes nothing more than a "Cain" offering.

So in chapter 7 of 2 Samuel we see a David who is so totally in love with His God that he wants to build Him a house. Now God hadn't asked David to do this, but something in David's heart wanted to express itself by doing something for the One he loved.

God's response was, "David, the way you have responded to Me is the way I'm going to respond to you. I am going to build *you* a house."

You will find that the house God built for David was not made of brick and stone. Rather, it was God's putting His favor on David's children and children's children's children. God said, "I know that I can transfer a curse, so how about a blessing? I will bless to a thousand generations."

It's about time for somebody from a difficult background to stand up in the name of Jesus and declare, "Divorce in my family stops here! Poverty stops here! Perversion and addiction stop here! Unbelief stops here! Instead of passing on more dysfunction in this nation, I will pass on a blessed generation that will perpetuate God's grace and kingdom."

PASS ON THE BLESSING

If I am successful but lose my children, then I am more of a failure than a success. If you ask me what the most important thing in my life is, I will tell you that, after my God, it is my family, and especially my children. They are more important to me than my financial security. They are more important to me than what you think of me, because they are an extension of me into the future.

> For such as are blessed of God shall [in the end] inherit the earth, but they that are cursed of Him shall be cut off. The steps of a [good] man are directed and established by the Lord when He delights in his way [and He busies Himself with his every step]. Though he falls, he shall not be utterly cast down, for the Lord grasps his hand in support and upholds him. I have been young and now am old, yet have I not seen the [uncompromisingly] righteous forsaken or their seed begging bread.
>
> —PSALM 37:22–25

You may be on welfare, and your family before you may have been on welfare. But I'm giving you a promise right now that you can take hold of: As the seed of the righteous, your children do not have to be dependent on a gallon of milk and a box of cereal from the government.

You can't go back and change the past, but you can

change the future. You can tell your children with confidence, "Sweethearts, you will never know the deprivation we came from; you have got a better chance because your mother is a daughter of God. There is a favor upon you because your daddy loves God."

The children of the righteous are blessed. That means your children and grandchildren have a greater favor working on their behalf than the children of those who do not have a covenant.

I tell my kids every day: "You will have doors open for you that won't open for an unsaved child. It's not because you're a white Anglo-Saxon with blue eyes and brown hair, or because you are an African American. It doesn't have anything to do with your grade point average, if you are the valedictorian of your college class or even if you never graduated at all."

Please don't misunderstand what I am saying. I am not demeaning the importance of having an education. I know of many who have all those things and still cannot find a job. I have unsaved friends whose children are Eagle Scouts, prom queens and football stars, yet struggle with drug addictions, low self-esteem, suicidal thoughts and the total loss of personal value and worth.

Six of the seven children my husband and I have are adopted. Some came out of horrible and even tragic backgrounds: welfare, teenage mothers, bigoted and angry biological grandparents. Yet, when they came into our home and became our children by law, we gave them not only our name, but also our covenant. Even the law of the land testifies to the fact that our adopted children enjoy the same rights, privileges and support that our natural child receives.

What an amazing testimony! Do you understand that as a legally adopted child of the King, you actually get to share in all the rights and privileges of your older brother, the heir to the throne—King Jesus?

Perhaps you have been told that your son is ADHD or that your daughter has the worst case of dyslexia her school has ever seen. I urge you to remember that when you gave your life and heart to serve and obey the Lord Jesus Christ, then out of that decision, that basis, you obtained an imputed favor over you and your family that those in the world do not have. Expect God to open doors for you that won't open for others. Favor is on you, but the seed of the wicked shall be cut off.

I was, no doubt, the worst geometry student in the history of the York County, Pennsylvania, school system—with the exception of Harvey Groveman. He made a jumping jack look like brain surgery (and it was just as painful, I assure you). He is probably the little guy who invented the little monkeys you make with socks and the silver diet suit that hooks up to the vacuum cleaner. You know, the one that is guaranteed to make you lose between fifty pounds ... or three and a half ounces, whichever comes first... by Monday morning. Just not *this* Monday. But I digress.

Geometry was invented by strange young men who wear their pants underneath their armpits, own only white sweat socks and count their plastic pocket protectors as a fashion accessory. Without geometry, I couldn't leave high school, so I tried earnestly to feign

126

excitement about the possibility of finding the area of a parallelogram.

My poor parents hired a tutor who gave me eight weeks of intensive study, which almost cost him his sanity, his salvation, and did I mention his sanity? I finished the course with an impressive low D. My teacher confessed, in a moment of frustrated professionalism, that he had given me the D so I would not have to repeat his class. The nerve of him!

So what is the point? My teacher, the tutor, my classmates and, at times, my parents saw failure. But because my mother and father built God a house, I received favor. That favor was not just for that class, however; God was directing my destiny to be mighty in the earth. It's in the bag, honey!

I can't moan over the past, but I can re-create the future—and so can you. I will not feel sorry for myself, and I will not blame anyone else—because I am not a victim. I have a destiny. I can overcome, and so can you. Just suck it up and stop feeling sorry for yourself. Make a difference! God is for you, and He will help you.

FAVOR FOR YOUR SAKE

How does God respond to the individual who says, "I want to built You a house"?

After King David died, his son Solomon came to the throne. We read in 1 Kings 11:9–13 that Solomon's behavior is incomprehensible, and God prophesies judgment on David's son ... except that God remembered in verse 12 that He can't do that.

God had made a covenant with David, and forty years after the old daddy king is dead, God says (and I paraphrase):

> Solomon, you stinker, you had better be glad that your daddy loved and served Me, because it would have broken his heart to have seen Me break you in half and hang you from that temple.

God delays judgment in Solomon's lifetime for his father David's sake. Some of you who are reading this right now feel as though you should have been dead. God spared your life when others better than you were taken, and you always wondered why.

You had someone in your life . . . a mother, father, grandmother, pastor or friend . . . who built God a house. Thus you received mercy when you deserved judgment.

Let's jump ahead fifty-plus years after David's death and see one of his great, great-grandsons on the throne. First Kings 15:1–5 tells us that this young man was Abijam. Abijam would have been history had it not been for the righteous life of David. It is *his* life that is preserving this bad seed fifty-some years after he is in heaven . . . all because he wanted to build God a house.

The way we sow is the way we reap . . . only much bigger and better.

Now let's go forward one hundred years or so into the future. (This is more exciting than a Steven Spielberg/George Lucas/Hal Lindsay novel.) God

YOU'VE GOT TO BE KIDDING,
I THOUGHT THIS WAS THE GREAT TRIBULATION!

128

couldn't, nor wouldn't, destroy Jehoram because of David. David, who desired to build God a house and invested millions in the kingdom of God, is still benefiting from God's favor; his children's children's children are receiving mercy they didn't deserve. It's all because of his simple gesture of love toward his God. (See 2 Kings 8:16–19.)

Then, some three hundred years after the worms have eaten David's body, an Assyrian general and an Assyrian king come against Jerusalem. Tiny Jerusalem doesn't stand a chance. But hear God speak through His prophet: "I will defend this city to save it, for My own sake and for My servant David's sake" (2 Kings 19:34).

God tells His people to go ahead and go to bed for a good night's sleep. He will send an angel to deliver this nation and save their king, who is a son of David. Remember, all David did was desire to build God a house, and God said, "I'll build you a house, David." One hundred eighty-five thousand people die some three hundred years after David died. David killed more people when he was dead than he did when he was alive! God is backing up David even in the grave.

RIGHTEOUS LIVING AND DECISIONS
PAY RICH DIVIDENDS

Your God has a great formula to meet your need. In chapter 5 of his Gospel, John tells how, when the angel of the Lord troubled the water at the pool of Bethesda, the first one to get in was healed. The second one to get in ... got wet. Basically, that means God has a timing for everything.

You are standing at a tremendous threshold in your life. If you continue to build His house, God has promised to take personal responsibility for you, for your house and for all that concerns you. If He has to, He will send an angel in the middle of the night to arrest that son, daughter or grandchild—even if they are forty years old and living on the other side of the world.

Keep building God's kingdom, and then ... go to bed!

Chapter
Ten

What Do You Mean,
God Is for Me?

> *We're still pretty tribal, when it comes right down to where the rubber meets the road.*

SOMETIMES STANDING FOR God means standing alone. How do we find the courage to do that, when standing alone may also mean standing against those who have elected to go another way?

In times like these, it seems that everyone opposes you. You sit out there all alone on a limb when you see someone coming. *Is that a saw he's carrying?* Things aren't looking good, but you're out there because you believe that's where God has called you to stand. Surely you remember the Scripture verse that states, "If God is for me, who can stand against me?" (See Romans 8:31.)

Somehow even that comforting verse doesn't help much as you look down from your limb into the angry faces of those who believe that you're actually a stumbling block, a troublemaker, even a rebel and an all-around pain in the neck.

Your soul goes through a lot of languishing as you consider the options. Maybe you did miss it after all; but then, you know God's voice well enough to know that you know that you know that He told you to stand right where you're standing. You also know it would be sin to turn back now.

So as the wind whips around you on your perch, as your opponents shake their angry fists up at you and as night settles all around, you draw your cloak tighter around you and turn inward. There you cling to God with the last strength you have left, as everything you knew, trusted and counted on for comfort suddenly becomes untrustworthy and very, very shaky.

For some reason, we like company. We're still pretty tribal, when it comes right down to where the rubber meets the road. We like to know that we're on the right track, with lots of company from like-minded people who see things our way and think we're great. But sometimes God calls us out to go it on our own.

It's lonely out there, and sometimes it's scary. Only when we know God's voice can we find the strength to make it through these times. In times of solitary standing, all alone on our own private limb, we can take heart that we're not the first who found ourselves alone against the world. Others have already "been there and done that."

Consider the story of the twelve spies sent by the Israelites to check out the Promised Land:

> And the LORD spoke to Moses, saying, "Send men to spy out the land of Canaan, which I am giving to the children of Israel; from each tribe of their fathers you shall send a man, every one a leader among them." ... Then Moses sent them to spy out the land of Canaan, and said to them, "Go up this way into the South, and go up to the mountains, and see what the land is like: whether the people who dwell in it are strong or weak, few or many; whether the land they dwell in is good or bad; whether the cities they inhabit are like camps or strongholds; whether the land is rich or poor; and whether there are forests there or not. Be of good courage. And bring some of the fruit of the land." ... And they returned from spying out the land after forty days.
>
> Now they departed and came back to Moses and Aaron and all the congregation of the children of Israel in the Wilderness of Paran, at Kadesh; they brought back word to them and to all the congregation, and showed them the fruit of the land. Then they told him, and said: "We went to the land where you sent us. It truly flows with milk and honey, and this is its fruit. Nevertheless the people who dwell in the land are strong; the cities are fortified and very large;

moreover we saw the descendants of Anak there. The Amalekites dwell in the land of the South; the Hittites, the Jebusites, and the Amorites dwell in the mountains; and the Canaanites dwell by the sea and along the banks of the Jordan."

Then Caleb quieted the people before Moses, and said, "Let us go up at once and take posses-sion, for we are well able to overcome it."

But the men who had gone up with him said, "We are not able to go up against the people, for they are stronger than we." And they gave the children of Israel a bad report of the land which they had spied out, saying, "The land through which we have gone as spies is a land that devours its inhabitants, and all the people whom we saw in it are men of great stature. There we saw the giants (the descendants of Anak came from the giants); and we were like grasshoppers in our own sight, and so we were in their sight."

—Numbers 13:1–2, 17–20, 25–33, nkjv

Ten against two—the odds were stacked against Joshua and Caleb who, when given a series of choices, chose to see good land, rich soil and lots of fruit. Because they knew that the Lord was on their side, they did not even let the number of the land's inhabitants, their stature or their fortified cities reduce the level of their faith. These two actually believed that they could prevail against any enemy . . . even giants. They saw themselves as "well able to overcome," while the other ten saw themselves—and all Israel—as "grasshoppers."

Consider how the two spies, Joshua and Caleb, must have felt when on their return to camp, their good report was overshadowed by the doom-and-gloom reports of the other ten. While the mighty men of faith, Joshua and Caleb, saw big grapes, lush land and great opportunity, the other ten saw menacing giants, danger everywhere and only impossibility.

The faith of the two was overwhelmed by the lack of faith present in the ten. Today's theology would attack Joshua and Caleb, taunting, "If you only had faith, there would be no battle! What was wrong with your faith that the ten won the debate? If you two had only had more faith, the Israelites wouldn't have had to wander around in the desert for another forty years!"

That kind of thinking just doesn't cut it in today's school of the Holy Spirit, where every confidence in the flesh is being stripped away. Sometimes it seems that God leaves us temporarily in the hands of our opponents. It may even appear that they're winning. We may have to reap the same consequences of their lack of faith when our faith stays strong. Where's the justice in that?

STANDING ALONE: A COMMON EXPERIENCE

Great men and women of God have been forced to stand alone at times. It's nothing new. Noah stood alone against all mankind alive on the earth in that

YOU'VE GOT TO BE KIDDING,
I THOUGHT THIS WAS THE GREAT TRIBULATION!

138

day. Only he and his family were spared from the tor-
rents of the great flood. Moses stood alone against
Pharaoh and even against his own people, who
remained stubborn and stiff-necked in the midst of
their promised deliverance. David stood alone against
Saul and his armies until the hand of God delivered
him into the place of his destiny: rulership over all
Israel.

Mary stood alone against social convention and
Jewish traditions as she carried the seed of God to
term. Joseph stood alone, against his own upbringing,
when he obeyed God's command to marry his fiancée
after she had been impregnated by the Holy Spirit.
Elijah stood alone against Jezebel's prophets of Baal ...
the list goes on and on through history. Even today
some of us may find ourselves forced to stand alone
against very real and very powerful opposition. But
know this: *Nothing that requires faith will be unopposed.*
Let's put that another way: *Everything that is of faith
will be opposed.*

Cheery thought, isn't it?

Just imagine how Caleb and Joshua took the news
when they discovered that the other ten spies who
had crossed Jordan had successfully squelched the
move into the new land. The lack of faith in those ten
spies, combined with the fear of the unknown, caused
the population to bolt and fall backward.

"Maybe we should stay put! Giants!"

"How can a ragtag band like us go up against giants?"

"Let's stay here! After all, we're getting manna
every morning!"

"No! Let's go!" countered Joshua and Caleb.

They were outnumbered.

The two men of faith were outvoted by the ten who lacked faith. Thus the two faithful ones were forced to wander for forty years in the wilderness alongside the faithless ones, even though they had courage and vision enough to cross the Jordan.

"Not fair," you say.

That's right, it isn't.

But sometimes God allows to unfold what seems to be unfair in order to work His higher, deeper and eternal purposes ... purposes that are hidden even from the eyes of the faithful and the visionary.

The faith camp would counter, "Those two men would have triumphed anyway if their faith had been strong enough!"

Randi and I have learned that sometimes even great faith is not enough to triumph against strong opposition. When such opposition comes, what do you do?

WALK IN THE SPIRIT

The Bible records that Paul walked in the Spirit. He often came to town with nothing but the clothes on his back, but he moved in such spiritual boldness and abundance of power that they carried him along, even amid great opposition. His uncompromised gospel message landed him in prison again and again. He stood alone against threats and revilings. But he stood fearlessly nonetheless, because he walked in the Spirit and put no confidence in his own flesh.

It's a good thing he was getting his instructions from the Holy Spirit, since today's church would have sent him first class, weighed down with lots of luggage and with the instructions to keep his message low-key so as not to offend the seekers in the pews.

Paul would have never gone for that. Sadly, the majority of men and women today who confess Christ do, however, walk in the flesh. They're easily turned away from the uncompromised Word because they are moved by the opinions of others. Threats cause them to quake. They are easily intimidated and turned backward. They're unstable and not fit for the Master's use because He can't count on them to obey no matter the cost ... even if that cost means standing alone against great opposition.

And opposition will surely come.

Get used to it!

Joshua and Caleb must have felt betrayed. Here they had risked their lives to go over the Jordan for a look-see. They had seen through eyes of faith, reported back and then had been scorned, reviled and made to sit down and be quiet while the other ten outvoted them. Then, because the Israelites refused to believe that they could go into the new land and subdue those giants, Joshua and Caleb were forced to partake of the same judgment as the unbelievers surrounding them. The people remained stubborn and unmoving, even though these two men were yielded to God and willing to submit. Their very testimonies were judged by the Israelites as untrustworthy and suspicious. Finally, no one even listened to their shouts of "We are well able to take the land!"

Can you imagine the amount of tension these two must have felt, not to mention the anger, at having to accept the same judgment as the rest of the tribe? Imagine how they must have felt, knowing that their testimony was not respected or even believed by their brothers.

It hurts when the people you live with revile you and attack your testimony. Even though God's grace is there to sustain you during such vicious onslaughts, the ones who most vehemently oppose you still seem to stand—and sometimes even prosper—while your every motive, word and action is examined under a microscope, then reported on for all to pass judgment.

It hurts, but God seems to be allowing it all to unfold. So what's next?

In times like these, the grace of God descends to help you stand against the most terrible opposition. As all around you begin to fall away, you stand ... alone ... unpopular ... suspect.

Still you stand.

What's the point?

Just when things seem to be the most impossible, God sweeps in and settles the score. That's the point! He likes to work in such a way that He gets all the glory. Maybe that's why He likes to let things get to the point of what I call "spiritual meltdown" before coming in, in all that glory, to set things right. Only God can move like that!

There are principles we can learn in times like these, if we'll just yield ourselves to God and kneel

You've Got to Be Kidding,
I Thought This Was the Great Tribulation!

142

low beneath His matchless hand.

PRINCIPLE #1

God's jobs are always bigger than you are. There are just some things so big that only the supernatural intervention of God can get you through to the finish line.

Ever felt like that?

That's how the ten spies felt—overwhelmed, hopeless, as if going up against those giants was just too much to ask.

But Joshua and Caleb possessed something called "vision." It enabled them to see the land, its fortified cities and menacing inhabitants through spiritual eyes. They saw that God had the ability to equip them with the supernatural strength to do the impossible. They put no confidence in the flesh. Instead, they trusted in God.

That's always God's way. He is constantly giving His people tasks too large and ominous to complete within their own might and abilities. Only when they bow before Him, acknowledging their weakness and asking for His strength to empower them, does He receive full glory for their victory.

He wants to make it perfectly clear that He's the one who fought the battle; we're simply the recipients of the victory.

PRINCIPLE #2

Anytime you step out with an action that requires faith, you're going to be opposed. Didn't I say that earlier?

It's worth repeating. Randi and I have learned this lesson again and again. In fact, I think by now we have a Ph.D. in this particular course. We're constantly stepping out in faith, only to get hit by the enemy's big guns. But we've learned not to put confidence in our flesh. We just keep doggedly pressing through, and God is faithful to give us the victory. Then, after the battle has subsided, He dresses our various wounds. The battle is, of course, the enemy's attempt to get us to raise the white flag of surrender.

Surrender at this late date? After all we've been through?

Not!

The ten spies in the wilderness also had seen God's miracles. They believed in miracles. They were fed daily by the miraculous hand of God. No, it wasn't that they didn't believe in miracles. They simply had no faith. They had no eyes to see. Their lack of faith meant lack of vision, and that led to doubt, discouragement, distrust, disobedience, disowning God and eventually to their destruction.

These ten spies opposed Caleb and Joshua. And when all ten had died, Joshua and Caleb were allowed to go over.

PRINCIPLE #3

Even though you're acting in faith, at times it may seem that God allows you to be overwhelmed. Why is that?

I honestly don't know. I just know that Numbers 14:20–25 tells how Joshua and Caleb were forced to

YOU'VE GOT TO BE KIDDING,
I THOUGHT THIS WAS THE GREAT TRIBULATION!

144

wander, the same as those around them who did not believe God's command to go take the land. It's easy to imagine their thoughts: *Why should we be punished for the unbelief of the other ten?* That's the hardest part of standing alone. You've stood in faith and given your all, serving God with all your heart. Yet for some unknown reason He allows the enemy to come in and overwhelm you.

I've learned, in my times of standing alone with God, that sometimes being right does not necessarily mean being victorious, or successful, right at that moment. Those things come later. Remember that the next time you're out there alone on the limb, being reviled and threatened by an enemy holding a chain saw in his hand.

You are where you are because God put you there. He can trust you there. He has a plan and a purpose, and even though you can't see it, it is nevertheless glorious.

Consider the great woman of faith, Corrie ten Boom. She called herself a "tramp for the Lord." She put her comfort and even her life on the line to hide Jews during World War II. She and her family, though Gentiles, where imprisoned in Nazi death camps. All Corrie's family who were incarcerated in death camps died there, except Corrie. Then, through a miraculous example of God's intervention, she was released. She spent the rest of her life traveling the world, telling of God's love and power to do the impossible.

She traveled alone.

One day, in a small church in Europe, a familiar

pair of eyes met hers. He had come for prayer ... and to ask forgiveness.

The eyes were the eyes of her Nazi tormentor—the one who had tormented and beaten her and Betsie, her sister. His cruelty had led to Betsie's death, and now he wanted forgiveness?

How could she?

Impossible!

Yet from that deep well inside her where the Holy Spirit resided, she found the courage and ability to do the impossible. Through Christ she could forgive, and she did. And the world was enriched as that powerful testimony went out from her.

Could you do that? Could I?

It seemed for a season that Corrie's tormentors had triumphed. Yet the very prayers she and Betsie had prayed in that camp had led to one of their captors' conversion. How could she not forgive?

Because she knew that God was in control, she stepped out and did the impossible. She looked in that man's eyes, and she saw Jesus.

PRINCIPLE #4

Let God deal with the opposition. Once judgment fell, Joshua and Caleb were silent. They said no more about those large grapes and that milk and honey. For the next forty years they wandered with the rest, trusting God for an outcome that would bring triumph out of the testing.

These two men of faith never ceased to believe that

God was in control. They waited on Him to prove that, and as a plague killed their ten counterparts, they alone survived to see the day when Israel crossed over Jordan and into the land of God's promise.

Be careful whom you allow to influence you during the times you're forced to stand alone. Although Joshua and Caleb stopped talking about their good report, they also refused to listen to the faithless reports of the other ten spies. God repaid the ten faithless ones, and the two faithful received a belated benefit: They crossed over and went in.

PRINCIPLE #5

Your job is to obey God, regardless of what others do. Ultimately He will vindicate you. Just wait. Part of discipleship means going it alone sometimes. God brought twelve spies into the new land, then gave them a promise and instructions. All but two disobeyed. Two stood alone, and they eventually received the promise because they served a faithful God.

And so do we.

Chapter
Eleven

Mature Christians, Not
Spiritual Know-It-Alls

> *Spiritual elitism goes along with spiritual pride, and pride always comes before a fall.*

SPIRITUAL MATURITY MEANS much more than simply knowing a lot about the Bible. It means much more than our being able to say, "I've walked with God for forty years!" Yet many Christians mistakenly believe that spiritual maturity is equal to spiritual knowledge and longevity. The longer we've walked with the Lord and the more knowledge we've accrued along the way, the more spiritually mature we are.

YOU'VE GOT TO BE KIDDING,
I THOUGHT THIS WAS THE GREAT TRIBULATION!

152

Right?

Not necessarily.

God is calling His people to become mature Christians, not spiritual know-it-alls. In fact, He's tightening up on us in some of these areas. Previously it seemed that He overlooked a lot of things—character issues, lack of spiritual fruit and so forth—if the person in question was still powerfully impacting the world by the anointing he or she carried. But I clearly heard the Lord say one day recently, "Cathy, I will no longer honor the messenger for the sake of the message!"

I tremble when I think about those words, realizing that these are no longer the good ol' days of "anything goes." Spiritual elitism goes along with spiritual pride, and pride always comes before a fall. Many Christians among us mistakenly equate the length of their spiritual walk, the amount of their knowledge, their high-profile status and the amount of "good" works they do with Christian maturity. But Proverbs clears that up for us; actions speak louder than words!

> Even a child is known by his deeds, whether what he does is pure and right.
>
> —PROVERBS 20:11, NKJV

Is all that "good" work watered down by the behavior of the one doing it? Is he or she on a private ego trip? Is that "good" work accompanied by occasional temper tantrums, with lots of foot-stomping, fist-waving and tirades thrown in? Or is the person walking in the outward manifestation of the fruit of the Spirit?

God is calling us up higher and into Christian maturity, a place in Him where some of us had not planned on going. The old gray mare ain't what she used to be, to put it bluntly, and these aren't the good ol' days. This is a new season, one in which God is watching what we do and say, and He is searching out our heart's motivations as never before. Consequently, we won't be sliding by on the "good works" excuse much longer.

SPIRITUAL MATURITY, NOT SPIRITUAL KNOWLEDGE

The humanist definition of spiritual maturity may mean "advanced spiritual knowledge," but that's certainly not the biblical definition.

Now, don't start getting defensive on me. I know that you're looking for more spiritual knowledge, or you wouldn't be reading this book. (Please don't stop!) I'm not suggesting that you stop learning, and I certainly don't recommend that you put this book down.

I'm simply suggesting that we reevaluate and redefine true spiritual maturity. To be spiritually mature according to biblical standards does not mean simply knowing a lot about Scripture; it also means having wisdom—enough wisdom to know what to do with all that knowledge in order to impact our world for Christ.

Uh-oh. I can hear some of you saying, "I bet she's going to bring up door-to-door evangelism next!"

Can't you just feel that "sloppy agape" oozing up off the page?

No, that's not what I mean when I say that we need to impact our world for Christ. Getting knowledge is quite a passive activity, really. Anybody can sit on a pew and listen to a sermon. To gain knowledge is to take in information. But to get wisdom is to gain the ability to appropriate that knowledge and find useful ways to dispense it.

I know, I know. Some of us would rather not be bothered with the brethren. We want to stay put in our "us-four-and-no-more" school of theology and let the fallen world fend for itself. I think, though, that Jesus meant for us to become more involved in each other's lives than is stated in the approach so popular today: "I love you, brother. Let's do lunch." Love means connecting on a deep level with another, not merely "doing lunch."

In fact, being spiritually mature requires that we love. It's not a "suggestive." It's an imperative.

THE IMPERATIVE OF LOVE

"In this the children of God and the children of the devil are manifest: Whoever does not practice righteousness is not of God, nor is he who does not love his brother," says 1 John 3:10 (NKJV).

Further, in verses 18 and 19, the apostle writes, "My little children, let us not love in word or in tongue, but in deed and in truth. And by this we know that we are of the truth, and shall assure our hearts before Him" (NKJV).

How I love Jerusha! I love her when she pleases me. I love her when she makes me proud to be her mom. I love her even when she disappoints me, and when she makes me mad I still love her. No matter what she does, I love her. That's how God loves us. It's how He would have us love each other. Now I can tell you that kind of love is not easy. It will require some death to self. We must have spiritual maturity if we are even to get close to loving each other with that kind of unconditional, steadfast love.

If we are ever to become mature sons and daughters, we must know the characteristics that mark such maturity. Let's look at what the Scriptures have to say.

THE QUALITY OF MERCY

Always remember that we reap what we sow. Each of us at some time or another has found ourselves needing mercy. Yet how merciful are we? Are we quick to forgive and extend mercy? Or do we exact payment of every last mite?

Isaiah 51:1 reminds us of our origins: "Listen to Me, you who follow after righteousness, you who seek the LORD: Look to the rock from which you were hewn, and to the hole of the pit from which you were dug" (NKJV). Only God can judge the righteousness of another. Only He can exact payment. It's our part to extend mercy, even when we may not feel like it. The mature saint is merciful, and so reaps mercy in time of need.

THE QUALITY OF HUMILITY

Isaiah 66:2 contains a powerful insight into one aspect of spiritual maturity: "'For all those things My hand has made, and all those things exist,' says the LORD. 'But on this one will I look: On him who is poor and of a contrite spirit, and who trembles at My word'" (NKJV).

O God! If only all Your people would tremble at Your Word!

We need a good healthy dose of the fear of God in this hour. Solomon, the wisest man who ever lived, recommended that: "By humility and the fear of the LORD are riches and honor and life" (Prov. 22:4, NKJV).

We *should* fear God. *He's awesome!* This God, who created all Earth's wonders—the majestic falls of Niagara, canyons, valleys, oceans, the splendor of ice-capped poles and tropical islands—is worthy of our trembling. Yet so many of us take Him for granted and treat Him like a great big Sugar Daddy in the sky. We buddy around with Him and cut deals with Him. We take a little off here and there, believing that because He loves us so, He'll make an exception. Then we find ourselves getting a little bit cocky, then a little more cocky. Then we get downright prideful.

A fall is coming right up ... the Bible tells us so.

Those of us who take the low way—who humble ourselves and fall on our faces in contrition before Him—are practicing an aspect of Christian maturity. We must continually examine how much our hearts still fear Him, for when we lose the ability to tremble before Him, we lose spiritual ground. Oh, that the very thought of violating God's covenant would make us tremble!

The spiritually mature son or daughter doesn't brag. Fools do that. Refer to the Book of Proverbs if you need a refresher course on the difference between the foolish and the wise. Proverbs 27:2 states, "Let another man praise you, and not your own mouth" (NKJV).

Amen.

THE QUALITY OF TRUTHFULNESS

The Word tells us how important this quality is. We must buy the truth and not sell it, for only then will we tell ourselves the truth. When we stop telling the truth, deception follows. The heart is desperately wicked, the Scriptures remind us. (See Jeremiah 17:9.) Who can know it? Only the searchlight of the Holy Spirit can keep our steps bound to the truth about ourselves.

The truth is, we ain't all that good.

The minute you think you're more spiritual than the rest, watch out! We need look no further than the Gospel of Luke to see what happens next:

> Two men went up to the temple to pray, one a Pharisee and the other a tax collector. The Pharisee stood and prayed thus with himself, "God, I thank You that I am not like other men— extortioners, unjust, adulterers, or even as this

tax collector. I fast twice a week; I give tithes of all that I possess." And the tax collector, standing afar off, would not so much as raise his eyes to heaven, but beat his breast, saying, "God, be merciful to me a sinner!" I tell you, this man went down to his house justified rather than the other; for everyone who exalts himself will be humbled, and he who humbles himself will be exalted.

—LUKE 18:10–14, NKJV

For some reason we don't like to bow before God—or anybody else—even though He is worthy of our bowing. We don't like to bow our heads in public. What will people think? Who cares? God sees everything. What *He* thinks is all that counts. When He looks down, will He see us as poor—bankrupt—in spirit and humble and contrite enough to bow our heads before Him? Or will He see us as modern-day Pharisees?

THE QUALITY OF WORSHIP

To be spiritually mature means to be a worshiper. The mature son or daughter understands the importance of worship. This individual does not have to be begged or cajoled into worship. It's a natural outpouring of his or her inner self. It's easy for this person to become humble before God and to raise heart and hands toward heaven.

The worshiper has already settled the issue of humbling himself before God. (See Psalm 95:6.) To worship is to both bow before Him and lift voice, heart and hands up to Him. These things require an act of the will to do them. Psalm 131:2 states, "Surely I have calmed and quieted my soul" (NKJV). We cultivate the stillness necessary to listen in the presence of God for the voice of His Spirit.

To worship God in all humility also means to be quick to repent, for when we get into His presence, we're convicted of our many sins and shortfalls. When we quickly repent, we can move on. If we don't, we may fall into pride, and from there it's a short trip on down the slippery slope.

THE QUALITY OF SERVICE

Finally, we need to examine our "profitability" to God. How's our service? Are we doing anything for Him? If we are, are we doing it for profit or out of purity of motive?

Service and faith go hand in hand. The greater the service is, the greater the faith. Yet many of us may be in danger of being written off as "unprofitable servants." Consider the parable in Luke:

> And which of you, having a servant plowing or tending sheep, will say to him when he has come in from the field, "Come at once and sit down to eat"? But will he not rather say to him, "Prepare something for my supper, and gird yourself and serve me till I have eaten and drunk, and

afterward you will eat and drink"? Does he thank
that servant because he did the things that were
commanded him? I think not. So likewise you,
when you have done all those things which you
are commanded, say, "We are unprofitable servants. We have done what was our duty to do."
—LUKE 17:7–10, NKJV

There are some things that, because we are commanded to do them, fall within the realm of what I
call God's "minimum down payment." These are the
things required of all Christians. True service begins
where duty ends. It costs something to serve the
brethren. (See 1 Thessalonians 5:11–14.) Mature
Christians have counted the cost and decided to pay it.
Will you?

Chapter
Twelve

Bald Women Have
No Bad Hair Days

> *Now here I was faced with the prospect of losing my lovely nails . . . all because of some black junk growing underneath them.*

I COULD SCARCELY BELIEVE **what I was hearing! It wasn't the end of the world; it was just a major blow to my pride.**

My long, beautiful fingernails had fungus. Well, they weren't actually my nails, but man-made fiberglass and tips that gave the illusion that my nails were a long, gorgeous masterpiece. I had worn them for years and had become accustomed to seeing them wave in the air as I taught the Word, made a poignant gesture or even shook a scolding, but well-manicured finger at a child. These nails had become a part of me and, I suppose, secretly a matter of image.

With a busy ministry, seven children and countless

important and mundane responsibilities, there is just not a great deal of time or resources for those weekend getaways to France or the French Riviera. So my nails were my luxury. My awesome friend Teri would graciously come to my house every other Monday, on her only day off, to pamper me for two hours.

Now here I was faced with the prospect of losing my lovely nails ... all because of some black junk growing underneath them. It was suggested that I obtain medicine from my doctor that would cure the fungus but also allow me to keep my nails.

I ran to the doctor. The conversation went vaguely like this:

"Dearest doctor, the most awesome doctor on the face of the planet, could you ... "

"No!"

"I haven't asked my question yet."

"Take your nails off."

"Boo-hoo. Can't I just have the fungus medicine?"

"No. The medicine that would kill this string of bacteria would also damage your liver."

"Do I really need my liver?"

(Sigh) "God bless you, Cathy. Go home and take off your nails."

(I know about the new fungus medicine, so please don't bombard me with literature telling me about this new cure.)

Unfortunately, I am ashamed to tell you, for about ten seconds I debated ... nails, liver, nails, liver. Now that is very sad. It proves what a premium we put on our image. Someone once said, "It is better to look good than to feel good."

As I stared at my doctor, she said incredibly, "You were thinking about keeping your nails on, weren't you?" I vehemently denied any such thing.

SMALL INDICATORS CAN MEAN BIG PROBLEMS

It took me a couple of weeks to finally do the deed. What convinced me was the information I read concerning the fingernail. I learned that many people look at the nails to determine a person's general, overall health.

In my case this was very bad. Isn't it amazing that something so small and insignificant can tell you about your body? Evidently mine were "abandoning ship," and my cells were putting on little life vests. The doctor told me that mine reflected the fact that this was not a nail disease, but a bacteria in the bloodstream that simply manifested itself in the nails.

I can't describe how it felt when she took those clippers and began the process of snipping my nails off. I asked her to wait a minute while I sang "Nearer My God to Thee." Snip, snip, snip ... off they came, one at a time! She told me that I couldn't even polish them; I had to leave them bare. Imagine that! They would have to grow out. When I asked her how long—one week, maybe two? She said, "A minimum of about four months." I began to hyperventilate. Four months! I would be hideous!

The doctor told me that she can tell how healthy a person is by looking at the nail beds. You know, that half-moon. Are all of you looking to see if you have any half-moons? You probably didn't even know you were supposed to own any.

When she removed my silk nails, there were no visible half-moons.

Is what others think about us so important that it interrupts rational thinking? Do you know that no one has even noticed that my beautiful diseased nails are gone? That is, no one outside of the friends to whom I had loudly complained.

YOU CHOOSE: LIVER OR NAILS?

Believe it or not, my friend, the Lord actually taught me something from my nail fiasco. I learned that I had some very strong ties to my image that I was quite appalled to see. I had temporarily thought of putting myself at risk just for the sake of my image.

Some of you have a fungus in your walk with God. He says that you have to get rid of those things and let your image go. It will only be for a season. He wants to purify you because the life is in the blood. You will have to choose between your liver and your nails.

What a valuable lesson the Lord was teaching me:

- Principle #1: We can carry disease and be totally blind to it.

- Principle #2: When it finally does appear, it just may affect our pride and our image.

- Principle #3: Shortcuts do not bring long-lasting

or godly change; rather, they eventually cause additional problems and pain.

• Principle #4: We must cry out for God's grace to embrace His will, even though it will temporarily be the most difficult path to take.

Let's see, your image or ... ?

You ask, "God, how do I do that?" It begins by your saying, "Everything I am and everything I have belong to You. I thank You that You want me to live and have life more abundantly. I'd rather be wrong doing something than nothing. I'm going to obey You, Lord."

The result? My nails are growing out all nice and pink and healthy at the base (and yucky at the tips). In a couple of months, I may or may not get nice, long, artificial nails applied to my fingertips. However, I can say that my nails have lost their once prominent place in my life.

This is my question to you, my beloved friend: Is there anything in your life right now that is covering up the disease?

Are parts of your image holding you back from the greater work of grace in your life?

ABSALOM, THE GORGEOUS HUNK, HAD AN IMAGE

> Now in all Israel there was no one who was praised as much as Absalom for his good looks. From the sole of his foot to the crown of his head there was no blemish in him.
>
> —2 SAMUEL 14:25, NKJV

I imagine that Absalom couldn't pass a mirror without looking at his reflection. This guy had it all, and he could have had his father David's whole kingdom. David had a special relationship with Absalom. The king must have admired his son's masculinity—and shared his white-hot temper.

I imagine that those around Absalom reminded him all his short, privileged life how gorgeous he was. No doubt the women swooned when he walked by, hoping that he would speak to them.

Although Absalom was not his father's firstborn son, he was still a prince. I suppose that he was an equivalent to England's Prince Andrew. Absalom had his father's good looks, but unfortunately none of his character.

After Absalom's sister Tamar was raped by his half-brother Amnon, the rage and hatred he felt simmered for two full years. (See 2 Samuel 13.)

When David found out what his son Amnon had done to his daughter Tamar, the Word declares that David was very angry, but that he did nothing. According to the commands of the law, Amnon should have died, for incest was punishable by death. (See Leviticus 20:17.) He was probably spared because David loved him, and he *was* the king's firstborn.

Absalom must have been watching and waiting for his father to do something. When he didn't, the anger in Absalom grew more intense. I imagine that David was most likely wracked with guilt over his own adultery and the mess he had caused.

David's lack of action must have created major

emotional problems for his children. By doing nothing against Amnon, David was just as guilty for seemingly condoning it.

I am a "grace" person. I want to assume that everyone will do what is right. I have been known to avoid confrontation at any cost. However, that only breeds confusion and multiplies the problem.

David just wanted the mess to "go away," but it didn't.

We must face our problems head-on, as difficult as that is. The mountain does not go away just because we choose to ignore it.

LEARN TO SAY NO

Amnon was twenty-two years old and the crown prince when he raped his half-sister. She was only fifteen years old. As far as she was concerned, her life as she had known it was over.

Because nothing was done to stop the disease, it just settled in a corner to breed and fester. Eventually Absalom turned his hatred for his brother into a plan.

The young man used the guise of a party, the sheepshearing celebration, to bring justice against his brother. When Absalom came to his father and asked his permission for all the king's sons to gather at his house in Baal Hazor for a little barbecue, his father said, "No."

David's reason for refusing permission was that hosting such a party would be too much of a burden on Absalom. However, David wasn't stupid. He knew

You've Got to Be Kidding,
I Thought This Was the Great Tribulation!

172

that there was bad blood between his boys, and he saw it as a powder keg. It also was a huge security risk to the throne to put all his sons together in one unprotected place.

That's the same reason they don't allow Prince Charles, Prince William and Prince Harry to all travel on the same plane. If it were to go down, the first three heirs in line to the throne would be in that big palace in the sky.

As our offspring often do, Absalom worked on wearing his dad down. You know, "Please, Dad, please, please, please ..."

I often see parents in Wal-Mart wagging their fingers in their children's little faces, saying, "No, you don't need another G.I. Joe or another Barbie doll. I'm not telling you again. No, absolutely not!"

Fifteen minutes later, mom is at the checkout counter. Her little Donna Sue has two new Barbie dolls, and brother has a complete set of G.I. Joe men and a jumbo pack of bubble tape.

A LACK OF WAR IS NOT NECESSARILY PEACE

What a pushover David was. Against his better judgment, he caved in and gave his son what he wanted.

Very bad move. If we take the easy route just to avoid conflict or because we are too tired to argue, we feed the iniquity in those whom we are supposed to be mentoring.

David's actions cost him dearly. Absalom had Amnon murdered, and then he took off to his grandpa's place for a couple of years.

David was devastated because he virtually lost two sons: his heir to death and his favorite to exile.

You might think that Absalom's having his revenge on Amnon would be the end of it. However, that is a trick of the enemy. Hatred, rage and murder come out of the root of unforgiveness, which is *never* satisfied.

Once again, instead of dealing with his son, David resorted to putting his head in a hole and avoiding the issue. Absalom took this as rejection, and the cycle began all over again.

What a dysfunctional family. When finally, manipulated by shame, David did agree to restore Absalom, it was too late. The prince's deceit was twofold. He stole the hearts of the people of Israel by professing his devotion to them; then he deceived David by professing devotion to God.

He was a proud, vain, angry and murderous young man who got by on his name, looks and charisma. It worked for awhile, but eventually it became his ruination.

The Absalom story was one of my favorite lessons in Sunday school. Those were the days before the punch-out flannelgraph people; all our flannel Bible characters had to be cut out with scissors. My Sunday school teacher was an eighty-year-old, half-blind lady. That explained why the Absalom character had not only long masses of wavy black hair, but also one foot and several fingers missing.

I can close my eyes and still see Absalom hanging from the flannelgraph tree by his flannelgraph hair.

My teacher then made Joab appear, riding in from the side of the board while eight little eight-year-old girls stared in wide-eyed disbelief as Joab stabbed Absalom over and over again. I think she was secretly taking out her frustrations in life on our little flannelgraph people.

As God begins to pick away at the fortress of our image, we need to give Him complete control. My nails were just an outward sign of something inside that was very, very wrong.

Absalom's hair was the outward manifestation of his pride, as a heavy growth of hair was considered to be a sign of great manliness and power. (He had his cut once a year; just read 2 Samuel 14:26.)

When the magnifying glass of God's precious Holy Spirit peers under our nails, our hair or even our incredible smile and dazzling personality and detects places of disease, God gives us initiative to help the process be less painful and produce a healthy heart more quickly.

Go ahead and confess your sins. Do not hide them. Hiding them usually leads to greater sin. Understand that continued refusal to deal with sin can lead to serious, even fatal consequences. Learn to see sin as God does. Seek to develop within yourself a godly hatred for sin.

I have to go now. I have an appointment to get my nails put back on!

Chapter
Thirteen

Will I Find Faith?

> *Whether it be God, flesh or the devil, wilderness experiences are still difficult to traverse.*

My HEART'S DESIRE WAS to write a book dealing with trials ... the little, baby, day-to-day trials and those huge, mountainous, all-consuming trials. Together, through these pages, we have explored the purpose of trials in our lives and how to maintain our sure footing when distressed beyond our natural limitations.

People frequently ask me, "Is this God getting my attention, or is this simply an attack of the enemy to discourage and discredit me? Or maybe what I call a trial is nothing more than living life in an imperfect world?"

Whether it be God, flesh or the devil, wilderness experiences are still difficult to traverse. In my humble opinion, the later the hour of God's deliverance, the tougher and more numerous those experiences become.

My purpose is twofold. First, I want to let you know that you are not alone. Second, I want to impart a sense of expectancy to you that lets you know your God's deliverance is very close at hand. I hope my experiences have encouraged you to trust that your God will never allow anything to come into your life without first giving His approval and providing a way of escape. Hallelujah!

There is one more thought I would like to leave with you as encouragement to continue in your journey with joy, even while all hell is breaking loose around you.

ALL PROPHETIC MINISTRY IS A MINISTRY OF RECOVERY

God does not intend for you to simply drag yourself across the finish line, but to dance across with His praise in your mouth and the spoils of war in your hands.

We have a mandate to protect God's image and reputation in the earth. It doesn't matter what obstacle we face or what situation arises. One day I was standing at the counter of McDonald's in the airport when the man next to me spilled his hot coffee. "Jesus Christ," he cried out, swearing. "Do you know Him?"

I asked impulsively. "What?" the man asked me with an annoyed and incredulous look on his face. "You said the name of my best friend, Jesus Christ, so I thought you knew Him."

He muttered something while mopping up his mess, then spinning around he made a hasty retreat. A believer who had been listening to our exchange of words from behind the counter suddenly went into a glory fit. "Praise God! Hallelujah! I love Him; I love Him!"

During the agony and ecstasies of life, we have a mandate to protect God's image and integrity in the earth. That is precisely why we must lose our image and allow His image to be seen in us. It is through the trials in our lives that we cry out to God. Thus little by little our image is replaced by His.

We are changed into what we focus on continually!

When we focus continually on our problems, we become consumed with our inability to resolve them. Then we end up anxious, irritable and filled with unbelief.

THE RETURN OF THE SPIRIT OF ELIJAH

There was a certain man in the Word who continually faced obstacles but who used every opportunity to bring recovery to all he met: Elijah. Malachi 4:5-6 speaks of the restoration of an Elijah-type ministry. The spirit of Elijah deals with the prophetic word and anointing. But what kind of a man was Elijah? What kind of spirit did this man possess?

YOU'VE GOT TO BE KIDDING,
I THOUGHT THIS WAS THE GREAT TRIBULATION!

182

We know absolutely nothing about him before 1 Kings 17:1. Here we see him in all the fullness and power of the Holy Spirit as he stands before wicked King Ahab with complete fearlessness.

We don't know anything about what it took to prepare and shape this vessel. We can only assume that before this mountain in his life, there was preparation in the valley. I call it the "pit of God's dealing."

The school of the Holy Spirit is a place where every confidence in the flesh is cut away. Before God can possibly take us before the pharaohs and kings of this world, we must always go through a period of preparation in obscurity. *God will use everything in our lives to prepare us.* He will use our marriage, job, ministry and even our failures to get us ready.

Of all the black-hearted, evil rulers, Ahab was the worst. His wife was Jezebel (we won't even go there). This queen had single-handedly seen to the execution of most of God's prophets. As far as Elijah knew, he was the only one left.

Elijah stood before Ahab and prophesied. He stood before this evil king calmly, fearlessly and boldly. He opened his mouth and said, "As the Lord liveth ..." That statement was the foundation of his entire life and ministry. What was the secret that enabled this man to walk right into the king's court and speak the word of the Lord, regardless of the outcome?

Maybe Elijah had found that place of intimacy and trust with the Lord that I yearn for in my own personal relationship with my God. Our Lord God will bring those who are willing, but the shaping of such a man or woman of God is not accomplished in a day. Nor does it happen at a three-day conference. It *only* comes through repeated hearing and repeated obedience.

As with Elijah, there have been plenty of times when God brought me to a place of security, provision and comfort. Then, all of a sudden, my world turned upside down and my brook of provision dried up. (See 1 Kings 17:5–7.)

What kind of a God would do this? It is a God who loves us, who teaches us that a little brook is not our source of provision. He is a God who wants us to look up, not down. He wants us where we have absolutely no dependence on the flesh.

He is a loving Father who wants to take care of us, even though at times we are filled with doubt.

HANG IN THERE!

My dear reader, the biggest temptation we face, when faced with a severe trial, is to turn to anything that will relieve the pain quickly. When you hurt either physically or emotionally, or even feel abandoned spiritually, the foremost thought on your mind is, *I want the pain to stop now.*

Millions of people run to bars, doctors, New Age gurus and even to Jesus looking for an immediate long-term answer to their hurt. More often than not, because of the influence of this fast-paced society that we live in, the person is left disappointed, defeated and disillusioned.

YOU'VE GOT TO BE KIDDING,
I THOUGHT THIS WAS THE GREAT TRIBULATION!

184

Even a "quick fix" from Jesus is certainly not a reality. That is why you hear so many people say, "Oh yes, I've tried God, but that didn't work either." It's because they were conditioned to take a drink, pop a pill, get a slap on the head by the evangelist and expect long-term, life-changing results.

It takes time ... time to cultivate a trusting relationship with your Father God. Even though He can touch you in an instant, it takes time for the wounds of life to heal. Just as there is risk of infection or relapse after a surgery, so we must give the Lord time to heal us after the heavy battles of war.

I know how difficult it can be. You can say all the right things and still feel hollow inside. But my friend, God, who began a good work in you, is faithful to also complete it (Phil. 1:6).

I continue to be amazed at the number of people who wait in line after I've spoken and ministered at a conference to tell me that they received one of my books from a friend or relative. Perhaps the title had gotten their attention as they searched the bookstore shelf at a time when they really needed it—at a time when the enemy had told them they were really awful, a failure or a disappointment to God. They feel that the Lord failed them, or that they didn't receive the answer they had prayed for. *Did God really love them? Did He really care about their suffering?*

We have become so used to "instant" answers or cures that we perceive anything that is not instant as rejection. No, my friend, it is exactly the opposite. I should know; it has been an especially difficult year for me. Yet I've come to know my Lord, my First Love in ways I never have before. I've come to know myself (which is sort of scary), and I've become more appreciative of the depths He will go to change me so I can better reflect His glorious image. And He will do the same for you. Therefore:

REJOICE, BE GLAD, BE HAPPY!

YOUR VICTORY IS A HEARTBEAT AWAY!

Covenant Ministries would like to
recommend the following taped messages by
Cathy Lechner

PICK UP YOUR WEAPON

HOPE IN THE WILDERNESS

FREE AT LAST

FROM DREAM TO REALITY

IT'S TIME TO CROSS OVER

HOW TO LIVE IN BLESSING AND GOD'S PROVISION

THE BATTLE IS YOURS

To order tapes
or to obtain more information on
COVENANT MINISTRIES please contact:

COVENANT MINISTRIES
P.O. BOX 17097
JACKSONVILLE, FL 32216
(904) 641-9880